Forward Press Poets 2009

UK Inspirations

Edited by Forward Press Editors

First published in Great Britain in 2010 by:
Forward Press
Remus House
Coltsfoot Drive
Peterborough
PE2 9JX
Telephone: 01733 890099
Website: www.forwardpress.co.uk

Foreword

Here at Forward Press our aim has always been to provide a bridge to publication for as many undiscovered poets as possible. We firmly believe that poetry should be accessible to all and most importantly should connect with the reader. Over the past 21 years we have published a hugely diverse range of poems from writers young and old, creating anthologies that celebrate the wealth of writing talent on offer. With the inclusion of both traditional rhymes and more modern verse, there is always something to suit everyone's tastes.

This latest collection of poems written with creative flair and a passion for the local area is sure to engage and entertain. We hope you agree that Forward Press Poets 2009 - UK Inspirations is one to treasure and return to time and again.

Contents

The Poems

Remember November 1918

Here I lie beneath
Cross and stone,
As I have done,
For more than sixty years;
Mourned by retired sentries:
Brooding with tear-brimmed eyes;
Scarcely muttering a prayer,
Or, stooping awkwardly,
To lay a poppy flower:
Shadows of comrades -
Replicas of youths,
Still stunned by:
A thunder clap, a muzzle flash,
Sight of blood,
- Mud, barbed wire;
Or blazing like the stars:
White eyes on black faces.

The call that brought us here,
Each year calls them back,
In remembrance of:
The eleventh hour, the eleventh day,
The dead;
The chime of a clock,
The peel of a bell,
Ringing out to:
Lid-tin heads, grimy faces,
Strained eyes, tired hearts,
Lean bodies and trench-soggy feet;
Ringing out
The soundlessness of peace;
A release
Second only to this earthy rest;
Where I await their final call
And then our memory will be tucked away,
Among some bookshelves
In a dusty hall.

Paul Conway

Through My Window

When in the morning I awake
I love to quietly lie,
And through my window gaze awhile
To watch the trees and sky.

In spring I see a fan of green
When soft the breezes blow -
A dainty, dancing filigree
Swaying to and fro -
A fan that flutters 'gainst a dress
Of beautiful, blue sky,
With a wisp of lace just here and there
As puffs of cloud drift by.

In summertime, their branches clothed
In voluptuous, bright array,
My trees join fingertips to make
A majestic, green archway.
Comes filtering through my pane the sound
Of birds greeting the day
As, darting through the leafy maze,
At hide-and-seek they play.

When the winds of autumn blow
And all the trees turn brown,
I see the gold and russet leaves
Gently spiral down.
And I see through naked branches
A seagull hovering there,
Poised just like an ivory brooch
Pinned upon the air.

Behind bare winter branches
In the cold, cold sky I've seen
Billowing big banks of cloud
With a river of blue between -
And I wait . . . and I wonder
If the river of blue will rise
And spread its flood-tide waters
Over the grey of the skies.

So my window frame's a speck of world
Of which I can never tire
While the Great Artist paints for me
Such pictures to admire.

Phyllis Hope

Place In My Heart
(This poem is dedicated to Patsy)

I look for you when the sun is rising,
You enter my thoughts as I awake.
Another day begins and I search once more.
I look for you when the birds are singing,
High up in the treetops out of sight.
Filling the silence with a chorus of comfort.
I look for you in the cotton wool clouds,
Floating further away out of reach.
Leaving the sky blue as they kiss goodbye.
I look for you in the colours of a rainbow,
When the sun is smiling against dark skies,
And the clouds are full of tears.
I look for you in the deep blue ocean,
The gentle ebb and flow so blissful.
As waves of emotion wash over the sand.
I look for you when the sun is setting,
Leaves dance in the cool evening breeze.
Casting shadows as the darkness falls.
I look for you in the brightest star,
Like a beacon in the still of the night.
But my hope is fading, I miss you.
I look for you from dawn to dusk,
In nature's beauty unseen by many.
So lost without you, where are you?
Then I look for you in a place so close,
Yet my eyes cannot see it, my heart.
And you are there, always were, and always will be . . . .

B D Nelson

Boppard

Boppard always set my soul to music
Boppard sets my soul alight today
In the music of the water
In the music of the highways
The spires of Boppard, the squares
The railway, the sunshine air
The river breeze
Mellow and tranquil, silent and private
Boppard has grown little today
Boppard is always the same
The soul of the river is seasoned by cruisers
By steamers and liners making their way
Dutch, French, German, Swiss to Arnhem, Bonn, Mainz
The soul of the river is embraced by the hillsides
The slopes of the vineyards
The slopes of the evergreens, the firs
Sing the praise of this watery place
The music of Boppard is bell-like and fine
The clock in the tower chimes, all is well
Boppard! Boppard! Boppard!

Margaret Bennett

Sun

The sunny days
Can cheer our ways
Into a rosy, cosy
Smile arrays
With its warm glow
Sparkle arrays
On sunny days.

D McDonald

A Village Demise

A little village near to town,
Was where we thought to settle down,
West Twyford, was the place we found,
With Guinness Brewery rambling round,
It gave us fields, a clubhouse too,
With cows on green land, what a view!
A church, a library and a school,
Five streets of houses, that was cool.

Somewhere to wander with the dog,
To take a ramble or a jog.
The children loved the atmosphere,
And all the time we were so near
To Hanger Lane with crossroads to
Go east or west - just up to you!
And then disaster came our way,
It was a really rainy day,

The football field was first to go,
With houses built all in a row,
The bowling green, the cricket field,
And parkland were the next to yield.
The easy access of our road,
To join the mainstream then was closed.
Our local library shut its doors,
Becoming flats of many floors.

And sadly then we had to sigh,
For Guinness Brewery said goodbye -
As brick by brick it disappeared,
A loss of something so revered.
The landscape changed, the village gone,
The friendships made will linger on,
But we have moved from what became
A built up suburb - *what a shame!*

Jean Goodwin

The Zodiac

Aquarius, the water bearer, blooms in January,
With their independent and honest ways.

Swimming into February, appears Pisces the fish,
Who are overwhelmed with emotion.

The sensational horns of March is presented by Aries the ram,
Assertive yet urgent, forthright, sometimes fiery and utterly
Enthusiastic with competitiveness.

Taurus the bull, charges through the month of April,
With patience, warmth and seductive romance.

May, May, the month of May for the twins of Gemini to appear,
Witty sense of humour, undoubtedly intellectual and always on the go.

The crab of Cancer descends into June,
Overcome with sensitivity, bursting with love but can sometimes
Be slightly moody.

The power and strength of Leo the lion erupts into July,
Extremely generous and confident, loving yet bossy but possess
Impeccable creativity.

Serenity in August with Virgo the virgin,
Undeniable intelligence, kind and hard-working with a
Critical eye and mind.

All hail the much needed balance of Libra the scales in September,
Concerned with achieving harmony, charming and easy-going
With a laid-back approach.

Scorpio the scorpion silently appears in October, private with a
Mysterious intensity, overflowing with sensuality, passion and jealousy.

Hitting the target in November is Sagittarius the archer, craving
Challenges and demonstrating their intelligence, philosophical and optimistic.

To end the year is Capricorn the goat,
Practical and extremely ambitious, disciplined and somewhat Prudent but have a
tendency to complain.

The endearing signs of the zodiac, describe our personality traits,
We are all unique and special so that the world is an interesting place.

Alicia Francois-George

My Soul Sleeps

My soul sleeps within all love's long gone
And every day my mind evokes the spirit's song,
Of those who loved then went their way
And those who would have stayed but passed away.
Now left bereft, alone each day,
I pray in cold discomfort and in pain,
For those I've known and look to know again.

Sad thoughts make sadder tears and inner strife
My time lived too alone encourages no more of love nor life,
That time passed, now washed away by solitude and inner tears.
My vanished joys bring me to be, throughout the years,
Beside myself without sweet company.

There is no relish now within my soul,
No brightness to my silent loves
But stays with me the memory of all that's worn,
Of love and family and of years, now left to mourn.
But all of us, though here or gone and from each other so apart
Will wait God's call to wake each sleeping soul
And fill again each empty heart.

Jeremiah Kelliher

How I Dream

I clean all day to earn my pay,
So one day maybe I may go away.
Foreign shores I adore,
If only one day I could afford.
I dream of a plane,
Or maybe even a train,
Either way,
I wouldn't complain.
But for now I will continue cleaning
This very dirty windowpane.

Lorna Ash

Closing Down

The closing down sale at the BBC
Was hosted by Wogan in the usual way,
With celebrity souvenirs being dug out,
Dusted down and put on display.

Cartloads of Chris Evans, Reeves and Mortimer,
Paul Merton, Angus Deayton, Jeremy Clarkson . . .
Dick and Dom, Rick Wakeman.

Signed photos from the EastEnders version of Doctor Who,
Signed photos from the EastEnders version of Robin Hood,
Signed photos from the EastEnders version of Merlin,
The list is endless . . .

And some rarely seen black and white photographs
Of loveable rogues Jonathan Ross and Russell Brand
In their early days as Oddbod and Oddbod Jnr
In 'Carry on Screaming'.

Robert Black

Summer Mourning

A string of bubbles slowly spiralled by
Round rainbow ribbons waving in bright sun,
A sign, I thought, from you to say goodbye,
A sign I'd sought that said, *it's time, move on.*
The empty anger and unspoken fears
Lodged in my aching heart, so long, were gone.
Each globe to me became a farewell tear
That burst, whilst I, transfixed, relieved, looked on.
So now the silent, raging question, *why?*
Unanswered by soft whispers of despair
Had ceased at last, you were dead, and now my
Grief flowed unveiled, in warm midsummer air.
I'd let you go, and through my tears I knew,
That was to be the last time I saw you.

Jill Gunter

September 3rd 1939

I remember, the place, the day, and the time.
Ramsgate, a Sunday, eleven-fifteen,
Third of September, 1939.

Mum and Dad, sat by the wireless, in the kitchen,
Of the Ramsgate house, of Uncle and Aunty Todd.
As the last hours of our holiday ticked away,
And the man, our prime minister,
Gave us bad news today . . . war!

I sat, and didn't make a sound,
Nursing a broken arm, wrapped in a sling,
Due to the very first day we'd arrived,
I fell down the stairs, the very first thing.

From seven years old,
I've carried this war wound of mine.
A scar from the plaster,
From the 3rd of September, 1939.

As we waited for transport, Uncle Fred's car,
My father and I walked the cliff top.
The white painted bandstand was empty,
A notice read, *The band will not play today.*
We looked over to France, a short distance away.

All was peaceful, on this beautiful day,
No sound of war.
Then came the sound of the siren, we wondered why!
When a solitary plane appeared from out of the sky,
We scurried for safety, my dad and me,
But the plane was a Spitfire, crossing the sea.

I remember Ramsgate, Sunday, a beautiful day,
The prime minister speaking,
Eleven fifteen the time.
And war was declared,
On September 3rd, 1939.

Frederick Seymour

An Extreme 70th Birthday

Your day must consist of excitement and thrills
Non-stop adventure with the minimum of spills.
So - we make a gallant start at the exact stroke of ten
A heart-stopping bungee jump off Big Ben.
Wow! Wasn't that fantastic?
Thank the saints for strong elastic.
Legs a little wobbly, knees a trifle weak?
Never mind, the colour is returning to your cheeks.
Now, off to Heathrow Airport and the busiest flight-path there
For a spot of hang-gliding, catch the thermals on the air.
Whoosh! Wasn't that exhilarating? And clever I might say
How you dodged and steered around that jumbo from LA.
I know you love a circus and the knife throwing act,
Well, this guy's a little nervous, but he's got a special knack,
Just stand where you're told to, you can show your fear,
The fellow with the knives won't mind, he can't see or hear.
Shaking now, and hesitant? But I still have more ideas,
Yes, it was a mite unfortunate that he pierced both your ears.
Ouch! Still up for fun? Juggling with
Flaming torches, that's a real hot one.
Not finished with the big top yet just listen to those roars,
You're booked next to put your head in the lion's angry jaws!
The hysteric laughter tells me you enjoyed that little wheeze,
What a mighty blessing the creature didn't sneeze.
This I think you'll like, of course it's just a hunch
It's pot-holing in the Chilterns (bring your own lunch).
Oh dear, you had a small landslide, well that wasn't planned,
But how kind of everyone to dig you out by hand.
Slightly caked with mud? Nothing we can't alter,
You'll clean up a treat when we get you in the water.
Free-falling over the Atlantic does take certain skills,
Oh my! You've turned a shade of green, just around the gills.
There's nothing here to worry you, it'll be over in a flash,
And there's someone waiting with a hook when you make that final splash.
Quickly onto water skis, shame that we were late,
They had run out of wet suits, that kind of sealed your fate.
In silky shorts and T-shirt I thought you were a goner,
Then I spied a figure, waving way out yonder.
On your return you seemed dazed and somewhat shaky,
Well, the day's not over yet, buck up and wakey wakey!

Before we leave the ocean and whilst you're still in shock
Summon up your courage, you'll need all the pluck you've got.
It's become a worldwide 'must do' I'm told it's all the rage,
Swimming with the sharks, did I mention there's no cage?
Okay, okay, perhaps not my greatest notion
But will you cease screaming now, you're causing a commotion.
The last event's more relaxing, it will feel just like Heaven
A full hour of mud wrestling with the All Blacks XI.
     Have a great day!

Doreen E Millward

Autumn

Soft, warm rain falling delicately,
Touching your face;
Bronze, yellow and orange leaves are shed
In that beautiful place - 'the woodland'
Where all is clothed in a ray of golden sun
To delight and stir the senses in you.
Berries of black and beautiful red
Dense in the hedgerows
Looking full and inviting, birds eat their fill
Thankful for nature's bounty, especially
Wild blackberries growing in the lane;
That autumn harvest is back once again,
Bringing a sense of well-being.
Evening shadows fall across the furrowed earth
As birds follow the plough, picking up
Their end of day meal.
All is well with the world.
The orange sun sinks slowly westward in the sky
And to God's beautiful autumn season
Once again we say goodbye!

Doreen McDonald Banks

Recollection

What lies ahead none can say,
Neither rich nor poor for the day.
We can speculate and plan,
Whether child, woman or man.
All that we intend to do
In the days, this year through.
Holidays, we plot and scheme,
Of exotic places dream.
Of marriage to our dearest love,
Hands entwined, glove to glove.
Then perhaps, of financial gain.
In sicknesses; relief from pain.
Comfort, of a friend in loss.
Knowing life's silver from dross.
Countless thoughts we can record
And errors, cutting as a sword.
Thoughts, concerning old loves grow,
All mankind throughout ages know.
Memory Lane recalls so clear,
Actions bringing many a tear.
Death must come to everyone.
Time preparations were done.
Repentance first, 'tis writ plain.
Eternity, with Christ, to reign.

Victor J Ensor

Follow The Light

Flickering candles of light
In quiet places of prayer,
Precious glass windows stained bright
Show saints and angels are there.

Thousands of shimmering lights
Held high by a joyful crowd,
Faith through the darkest of nights,
Sending their blessings out loud.

Millions of stars made of light
Twinkling in the night above,
People amazed at the sight,
Hearts overwhelmed with the love.

Creations made out of light
Leading the way through the dark,
Keeping the true goal in sight,
Making each good deed a spark.

Follow the way that is light
That leads us all safely on,
For in the dark of the night
It shines for everyone.

Gilly Jones

Big Ben's Bong

In the year 1859,
Big Ben's bong begins to chime.
He looks down from his tower on high
At the faces looking up to the sky.
His bong echoes through London town,
While tourists watch from the ground.
Every hour on Big Ben's bell,
The hammer strikes the time to tell.
Bong! Bong! The hour is clear
From below all the crowds cheer.
We set our watch by Big Ben's bong,
The time he tells is never wrong.
Even the BBC, his bong they use,
Nine big bongs, it's time for the news.

Rita Pedrick

Remembering Isabella

Dear Carol, I know this is a difficult time for you,
And I just wanted to let you know how much I love you.
I know we'll always remember Isabella forever,
And losing her has brought us closer together.
Now you've got Kamran, your beautiful baby boy,
And I know he'll always be your pride and joy.
I really do think you're a brilliant mum,
And one day you may have a daughter as well as a son.
I'm glad Kamran loves his Horace the bear,
I really love Kamran, as I know you're aware.
Just wanted to let you know I'm thinking of you,
And Isabella is with you in everything you do.

Anne Voce

Remembering The Days

Understanding the world around us.
In so many different colours.
From birthdays to birthdays.
People to people.
Finally, got my eyes fixated
On a heart of gold.
Over the rainbow,
With marshmallow clouds
And pink champagne,
And blue waters of happiness.
Forever the smiles, love and joy.
Was like a dream.
Sweetheart of my own heart.
Dream of my own dream.
Painted pictures of colours gone by.

S Beatrice Ally

Dear John

I wore my United kit that day, considered all round a good choice
A day to laugh and cry, and even, the minister said, to rejoice
But a visit to school was in order first, though some said it was quite inept
Then out onto the open road, and family and friends, how they wept
I was bumped about, then settled down, in church, in some dark place
Hymns were sung but thinly, my parents in one loving embrace
Was I really Mum's little soldier, the bravest in the land?
The minister tells the congregation how I lent a helping hand
I couldn't let my brother drown, and with all my strength pulled him out
From that murky water, but I fell in and no one heard Danny shout
Dear Lord, it's getting hot in here, all have said such kind things about me
But it's time to go now, I'm at peace
Dear Danny, I hope, so is he.

Jillian Megram

The Hairdressing Salon

Somewhat like birds' feathers, they floated and fluttered and fell,
Favourite, feminine, flaxen locks, in a fluffy spell;
As they cascaded silently and slowly to the floor,
Flowed also, in sympathetic drops, tears of one who saw
Many years of patient brushing, and tender loving care,
Now the discarded detritus, of a shorn head of hair.

With neither feeling nor mercy, still scissors in her hand,
The mercenary hairdresser cuts, as if by command,
Holding, fondling, caressing and combing through the tresses,
Totally oblivious of the owner she distresses,
Swiftly and silently slicing, ruthlessly, through the strands,
The long, woven, golden braids, of severed hair in her hands.

Then the young assistant, armed with brush and bustling haste,
Sweeps away the evidence, to a pile of hairy waste,
Mixed with darker clippings, from a streaky redhead perchance,
Who only needed trimming, her appearance to enhance,
Amidst the smell of shampoo, and acrid, stifling lacquer,
Superfluous extensions, of grey, or brown, or blacker.

Just in time, the victim cries, to save a wee example,
To be rescued, for the memory; one golden sample,
That will lie locked away in a casket many years hence,
A reminder of the fateful day, when her common sense
Reluctantly suggested, to the hairdressing salon,
They cut her hair from shoulder length, till all of it was gone.

Ian Boddy

The Trap

There's always a star whose beauty did glow
Trying to stay like she was long ago
And prepared to accept the pain of the knife
Afraid she'll lose out to a much younger wife
In her mind she's the beauty she once used to be
A trophy her husband wants others to see
And while it all lasts, she's Queen of the May
But if it should fade, his attention will stray
As each day we read of a name from the past
Of some ageing star whose looks did not last
The picture in close up, still in the grand dress
Shows us a face, now long past its best

Beauty they say you just cannot buy
But desperate women are willing to try
So after the face has been lifted and cut
And the chin or the nose or cheeks do not butt
And silicon implants have enhanced the frame
For another small fortune it's all done again
Till all of a sudden, no more can be done
And one rich man's wife became a figure of fun
That glamorous life is now yesterday
The false friends are gone that she met on the way
For now that her beauty is showing the strain
She's left with her dreams and tears and her pain.

Charles H Boyett

Comic Wit

Comic wit?
I hear myself
Speak out loud.

Every wave of your
Expressive hands wafts the air
As you stride in
And bow to the waiting crowd
As they applaud you in
Your absolute glory
Of wild, back-combed hair
To your drainpipe, black, tight, stretch trousers
As you stand brave and bold.

And I do declare that there is an air of deep love for humanity
That springs from your conscience there
That allows you to balance out your soul
Oh yes, I have seen your act
And have sat with my mouth ajar
'You can't say that,'
And a nervous laugh follows as I breathe in the air
How light my heart
Giddy with laughter
And for a short while
I lose myself within your speech
Your thoughts
Your eyes
And the way you see the world.

And although in jest I know
Your comic wit is not always light
Some heavy stuff is tossed in there for good measure
That jolts the crowd, hear them protest a smidge,
With 'Eh!'

Anetha Hunte

The Joy Of Verse

The joy of composing poetry,
At least it's this way for me,
It's when others get joy from reading my work,
That's my reward you see.
If nobody ever read the poems,
Then all of my effort it totally wasted,
Like a master chef creating a banquet
And none of his food is tasted.
An artist or sculptor should fare the same,
If their creations were never seen,
Without their wonderful works of art,
It would be as if they had never been.
What a sad little world this planet would be
Without the visual arts,
Where would we find the stimulation
To excite our minds and hearts?
Don't get me wrong, I'm no William Shakespeare,
Wordsworth, Shelley or Blake,
I only write as it gives me pleasure,
To think any other would be a mistake.
If I write a poem for a special occasion,
For a relative or friend,
If what I create gives joy to them,
Then it's worth it in the end.
Finally its publication, set in print,
In a well bound book,
Like a nugget of gold to be discovered,
Should anyone care to look.

Geoffrey Alan Chapman

Dreams Of A Dormouse

Even when the sun gleams high
Amid the cloud ships in the sky,
And nature agitates with life,
The dormouse dreams.

Even when the blackbird sings,
Butterflies extend their wings,
And adders rustle through the grass,
The dormouse dreams.

Even when the summer breeze
Uplifts the dust about the trees
And woodlice scurry under stones,
The dormouse dreams.

Even when the farmer's gun
Excites the rooks and rabbits run,
And Mrs Tinker beats her rug,
The dormouse dreams.

Even when the day nears night,
And bats enjoy the losing light,
While moths embark on quiet patrols,
The dormouse dreams; then stirs.

Francis E Adams

Pedestrian Precinct

'Do you know where they've put the bus stop?'
An old lady said to me.
'I've been up and down and round about
But I'm hanged if I can see.'

Why do they have to change things?
What's wrong with the way they were?
If my old mam could see it now -
Why, she'd turn in her grave, I'm sure.

And when they built that bypass
Why, I couldn't believe my eyes
That big hotel at the top of the hill
Seemed to have moved to the other side.

See this pedestrian precinct
Have you ever seen so many bricks?
It must have cost a fortune,
Just looking makes my eyes play tricks.

And don't ever try to drive here
When I drove down t'other day
A man was frantically waving
Go back, you're going the wrong way.

So what with the pedestrian precinct
And the system going one way
I think I'll shop somewhere else now
Via the new dual carriageway.

M Jackson

An Old English Fable

There was a lady by a lake
And a magic sword she did make.
To a wise wizard she was wed
But she shared an old king's bed.
She had a daughter then a son
In later life they would have great fun.
Become the stars of an old English fable
About a king with a round table.
The king did carry that magic sword
And ruled the land so far abroad.
That daughter cast a magic spell
And had a son the story did tell.
The king fell for a queen from France
Who loved a knight with a lance.
The daughter had the king's desire
And did burn inside like a dragon's fire.
With strong wine that king got merry
Brought down his throne in Glastonbury.

Colin Allsop

A Stroll In A Field

There are numerous items to catch the eye at a car boot sale,
Crowds travel the countryside to sell and to buy,
Plants for all types of gardens, colourful flowers for gifts,
Piles of clothes and shoes, both old and new, for you to sift.
Home-grown fruit and vegetables, all organic
Are displayed next to a stall displaying items mechanic.
Home-made preserves, sweets and cakes, jostle with books on
Keep Fit and Pilates.
Toys by the dozen on every stall and what is more,
Prams, carry cots, any item for babies can be bought.
Furniture too, antique and new, is proudly displayed
By brick-a-brac stands where jewellery is arrayed.
Home linens and hobbies, knitted garments to view,
Ancient tools, old walking sticks, fishing rods any for you?
And what do you think? I have even seen an old kitchen sink!
All this and exercise too, I don't think there is more you can want,
Do you?

J E S Kain

Birthday!

Congratulations, 21 today
Make your dreams come true
For only you can
Your wishes are blessed
By angels indeed
Stars in your eyes
Bright as can be
With so much hope
Whispers in clouds
Smiles in the sky
Smell of summer in the air
Just daydreaming
Birds sing to you
Butterflies flying in the air
Clouds drifting like pillows
Doves kissing
What a lovely sight

Smell of the grass being cut
It must be summer indeed
The bees making honey
What a lovely taste to share
Smell of chimney smoke
The fields are so golden, like gold
They shine like money for the harvest
So strong indeed
Deer in the fields grazing
Hares skipping and jumping
Rabbits eating the long, lush, green grass
Crows in the fields pecking
Blackbirds watching from above
Sparrows sing their hearts out
Pigeons flirting

Hens laying eggs, what a lovely sight to see
Baby chicks all around
Cows grazing in the fields with their calves
Horses with their foals
Pigs with their piglets
Ducks swimming in the pond with their ducklings
Swans in the lakes looking like angels
Otters playing like children having fun

Kingfishers catching fish for tea
Hedgehogs vulnerable as can be
Frogs hopping, grasshoppers jumping
Crickets talking, flies flying, wasps buzzing
And the scarecrows just stand there quiet as can be.

Lindsey Way

Goodbye Dear Friend

Words cannot express, dear friend,
The pain I feel today.
Saying a final goodbye to you,
Fills me with dismay.

Friends since we were young,
Supporters of each other.
You understood my thoughts,
Were like a second mother.

Our friendship stood the test of time,
Throughout life's toils and troubles.
No one could come between us,
Nor burst our perfect bubble.

Whenever I felt down,
You were there to pick me up.
Laughter, sunshine followed you,
Love overflowed my cup.

Now, I must be strong for both of us,
As clearly I can see,
Death is not the end, my friend,
There will always be you and me.

Marion Brown

It's Your Fault

I wrote a romantic poem for you to change into a song
And went with you for four years until you said so long
Up 'till then that was the best four years of my life
But I left you for causing me so much grief and strife
And now I say I don't even miss you the slightest bit
But deep down inside my heart I've just got to admit
Maybe I shouldn't blame you because the fault is mine
Or maybe it's your fault because you made me pine

I remember the first Thursday night we met in the hall
You were five foot one and made me feel ten feet tall
I fell in love with you because you were so exciting
Even today I'm recalling this with what I'm writing
I guess that I could say I loved you then I suppose
But after a couple of years the Thursday club would close
I heard the bad news and I really felt so blue
But I couldn't say it's your fault because it wasn't true

I still came over to Sandyhills although I didn't have a car
But I still took you out to dinner or Kimberley's bar
We held hands and did all the things that lovers do
And we went to the cinema to see a movie or two
I've been reading an old diary to see their names
Lethal Weapon Three was first, then Patriot Games
One starred Mel Gibson and one starred Harrison Ford
And maybe it's your fault because I was getting bored

We met at the Gesh a month or two after that night
I was so glad to see you and I held you so tight
I remember how I thought you'd never let me go
I can recall every detail although it was so long ago
But our happiness only lasted a couple of years more
Because you did something you've never done before
You broke my heart by cheating like it was a game
It's your fault, you've only got yourself to blame

I remember Margaret asking me to give you a chance
But God help Chris if she caught him making an advance
I heard Michelle telling me she thought you're a maddy
She'd caught Gary cheating and started going with Paddy
I heard Debbie's relationship with Stuart was in doubt

They were always arguing and he was on his way out
Now Rosalind, there's only one more thing I want to say
That it's your fault entirely that I left you that day.

Andrew S Gibson

Ode To A Lamp Stand

Hauntingly, you crowd my space!
With telling force,
A'tween my vertical curtains
You illuminate those darker ways
Assassinating those shadows
That lurk and creep
O'er Pembury's quiescency
As falls the evening dusk . . .
'Neath your canopy of light
You generate that power,
Seeking out those portraits
Of yesteryears, forever foraging
Those erstwhile whatnots,
Ere grief or play.
Durst do I liken thee to
Some robotic presence
Your tall avant garde posture
Does dutifully obey!
Shine on lamp stand!
Give light to those more
Memorable times . . .
Activate some quixotic dream
Of sparkling power!
You cast no laughter, nor tears,
Yet furtively, you awaken those
Hidden passages of time
Giving radiance wherein
Such dreams and romance,
Sweet and tender thoughts allay.

Terrence St John

Cameos

Cameos of life
Cameos of love
Falling rose petals
Cascade from above.

Whispered sweet nothings
Caress the stage
Cameos of time
Twenty-one years of age.

Twenty-one years
For cameos to shine
Please raise your glasses
Champagne and wine.

The cameos of life
Thank you forever today
As their whispered sweet nothings
Forever embrace yesterday.

Geoffrey Meacham

Woodland Fancies

Sitting in the shade awhile
On a fine spring day,
I can see at least a mile
Of woodland bright and gay.

Children darting to and fro,
Between the trees so green,
Playing games of peek-a-boo,
Oh, what a happy scene!

Mothers with their tiny child
Making sounds of glee,
Dogs and cats a-running wild
Happy to be free.

And frogs a-croaking in the stream
And butterflies galore,
Dragonflies with wings that gleam,
And so much more and more.

If I could stay forever here,
How happy I would be,
But now it's time to go back home
To mother's home-made tea.

Carolyn Aryaeenia

Breaking Through

Quietly sat in her corner of the grey space with no soul,
Very aware of her small part in the department, the whole.
And somehow different from others, no burning ambition,
As judged by their standards; instead, her own thoughts, her own mission.
No desire to jostle for position, achieve to excel,
Always in the minority, just needing to do well
And stay true to herself, be honest, put food on her table,
Her team and the managers knew her as willing and able.
Until the day; she could take the smart lip service no longer,
And found courage to speak up, as her convictions grew stronger.
Closed ears listened to her, but far too busy to really hear,
This unusual honesty caused some to face their own fear.
She'd soon realised that her efforts would never be enough,
And she also knew she could not go on being that tough.
She wore more and more make-up, as she got depressed and more stressed,
On the face that did not fit; she could not see it, as she dressed,
So, side-lined; now where was her team? 'Stay strong, we must keep in touch,'
After two months it was obvious they did not care that much.
They'd got used to her empty corner, where her plants wilt and die,
Too embarrassed to discuss her absence, this sickness; and why.
Her critics continued, 'A good worker, but aloof and proud,'
'Couldn't take the strain, bound to happen,' 'She left under a cloud,'
But beyond their dim views now, and walls of dubious grey hue,
She finally returned to the real world, where she found the sky blue
And maybe one day some of them will feel that they have no choice,
No more compromise, or lies; and give integrity a voice.

Adrienne Young

They Didn't Walk Alone

Joy and happiness overflowed
As fans came there in many bus loads
Outside the crowds grew thicker and thicker
While things inside were very much quicker
The whistle blew and the game got a start
But outside the gates they were breaking their hearts
Police with those fans didn't know what to do
As everyone pushed and tried to get through
By now there was fear outside those gates
People were crushed by each other's weights
Then a voice gave the order to open the gates
Not knowing the stadium
No more people could take
For 96 fans they were gates to Heaven
Because they died in the rush
To see their favourite eleven
So the joy and happiness that started that day
Ended in sorrow along that fateful way
The field where that game would have been played
Became a carpet of flowers for the next seven days
And thousands of people passed that way
To pay tribute to those who died that day.

Ellen Walt

Fat Little Old Me

Is it just me
Or are others frustrated
With being told they're overweight?
Those extra pounds, by me are much hated.

I'm fed up with being reminded
By health freaks on TV
Less calories and more exercise
Will help obtain a slim new me.

Suffering from thyroid and food allergies
For me there must be little hope
My doctor and dietician can do little more
I try to stay mobile, but being disabled, it's hard to cope.

When young, I was slim and athletic,
Always on the go,
Now a pensioner, those days are gone,
Less mobile now, I sort of trudge instead of flow.

Strange, I'm happier now,
Than I have ever been,
Don't feel I have to keep up with style,
I'm me and don't care at being seen.

So lay off you lucky skinnies,
Some people can't help being obese,
It's not a perfect world,
So let your criticisms cease.

Ann McAreavey

Night Of The Storm

The night of the storm
Took us all by surprise
I slept through it all as the gales rushed by
Uprooted the trees as they came tumbling down
Trees that have stood for years in town
In the country they were not spared
Breaking, groaning, trying to bear
The force of the gales as they stood so supreme
Majestic and tall and still the gales screamed
Then they succumbed and finally fell
One after another it was sheer Hell
The farmers all suffered a terrible blow
They looked all around, and just did not know
Which way to turn or what to do
Their crops all flattened and apples too
Were torn from the trees and strewn around
The farmers' life's work has gone to ground
The trees at Kew Gardens, the beech and the oak
Were lifted like matchsticks and felled with one stroke
But now it is over one must start again
Plant the young trees in place of those slain
And when they have grown to their beauty and height
All will be forgotten of that terrible night.

G Antignolo

Violin Serenade

From a high balcony overlooking some woods
I hear the sound of a distant violin
Playing a serenade to an unseen lover;
And, as dusk falls and all becomes hushed,
Creation seems to hold its breath,
As if to listen in rapt contemplation
To the purest, most exquisite melody
That has ever graced Nature's repose.
In imitation of the nightingale's song,
The violin fills the still night air
With tender harmonies which, quivering, rise
Out of the softly descending silence
Of the rich-scented summer evening
Like a crystal fountain spring arising
From an invisible and soundless source -
Harmonies which, heightened by trills and tremolos,
Soar on wings to highest Heaven.

I climb down from that balcony hung
With honeysuckle and sweet-scented jasmine,
And cautiously approach the unknown fiddler;
And only now do I faintly hear,
Singing divinely in the sylvan background,
The gentle, ceaseless murmur of a flowing stream
Providing the violin with accompaniment serene
Deep within the sleeping woodland.
Sounds of heavenly music combine
With the summer evening's fragrant balm,
Until Creation itself seems to be singing
A serenade to the great Creator Spirit -
A blissful nocturne of ecstatic rejoicing.

And now, it seems, the heavens open;
And from the shining firmament hung
With myriad golden-branched constellations
There comes a music so divine
That it seems to descend in showers of silver -
A music of the purest melody
Transcended by the sweetest concord sublime,
Played with citherns finely strung
And on virginals divinely tuned,
Accompanied by a celestial choir

Echoing a distant antiphon
In remote realms of infinite splendour,
Singing of that universal harmony
Proceeding from the Fount of Love.

Long into the dreaming summer night
The solitary fiddler plays his violin,
Creating the most beautiful sounds
That have ever spanned the boundless ether
And stretched beyond its loneliest confines;
And as the unending song of love,
Soaring higher and ever higher,
Finally reaches the eternal Throne
The Gates of Heaven seem to open,
Revealing the wondrous glory on high -
Glory which surpasses human conception
And far outshines all mortal thought.

Play on, violin! Play on!

Robert D Hayward

Cattle

Unlike us, you are trusting, simple,
Your brains are calm.
Excited not by greed or lust,
You exist content,
Happy with pasture and company.

The sheeny softness
Of your hair, betrays your yearling state;
Shambling to meet us,
Soft-hard bodies jostling at the gate.

Humble yet exact,
Flicking off flies from steady backs.
Acquiescent gazers,
Lunging strange to our proffered hands -
You cannot live for long.

Sylvia Lees

The Season Of The Fall

The stars shine brightly in the skies so clear
And the moon wears a halo hinting winter is near.
A touch of frost is in the air
And a cool wind blows everywhere
The conkers are falling from the trees
Not far behind are the turning leaves
Their colours show a stunning view
With their red and gold a warming hue.
There are berries now appearing on the trees
The winter famine to appease.

In the garden dahlias shrivel in the dawning light
After the frost has nipped them in the quiet of night
The winter pansy may resist the chill
If only for show and the strength of will
All the gardens now have a chance to change
And without our help nature will rearrange
The lawn once so lush and green
Turns a dusty brown, no life there to be seen
The worms are burrowing far below
Leaving hills of soil where your footprints go.

Some birds soon will turn to flight
A warmer climate is their right.
The starlings soon will be no more
In a distant garden they will cause uproar
The bees and wasps, all their source of sweetness gone
Disappear in silence, all their work is done
All the birds and animals alike
Will watch and wait the cold to fight
With nature's help they will survive
New life will be born and the old revive.

Sheila Storr

Mary's Picalax Journey

They gave poor Mary medicine which makes you really 'want to go'
So she spent all day on Thursday trotting to and fro
She'd been ill and they had given her the dreaded Picalax
Which is a horrid, cruel medicine which caused her to make tracks
Across the floor of Gossip ward, twixt lavatory and bed
Until on Thursday evening, the poor girl was well nigh dead.

But Friday morn was different, she was filled with putrid air
Which burst from certain parts of her and made the other patients stare
Some raised their eyes to Heaven, and gave her meaningful looks,
Others shook with merriment and hid behind their books.

Poor Mary now felt terrible and was dreadfully embarrassed
She said she was ashamed and began to feel harassed
So she went into the corridor to try and ease the tension
And was suddenly aware of a new and strange sensation.

She rose up in the air and seemed to glide across the floor
Unfortunately someone had forgot to shut the door
She was jet-propelled immediately like a shot out of a gun
Above the fields and rivers, quoth Mary, 'This is fun.'
Her heart sang and her soul soared as she sailed across the trees
And birds gasped in sheer amazement as did the butterflies and bees.

Now all this time her lovely son, who is a really Gorgeous Beast
Decided to visit Mary and drove north then slightly East.
And looking up he suddenly saw sweet Mary's frilly drawers
As silently and happily along the A30 she soared.
'Hey Mum!' he cried in terror, alarm, fear and dread
As disbelievingly, he slowly shook his tousled head.
'Hi, son!' she shrieked at him, then shouted very loud,
'Goodbye my darling boy,' and, she disappeared in cloud.

So ended Mary's earthly life and the Gorgeous Beast still tells the tale
Of Mary's Picalax journey, as he sups his jug of ale.

Priscilla Sharp

World Of Creation

Simply wonderful news
Surpassing all blues
Welcoming folk to a vast community
Of poets contentedly expressing poetry
World of creation the pen circulates wide
Folk fascinated with open eyes
Captivating poetry through veins tingling
Mind in rhapsody sets thee thinking

Writing poetry be a pleasant pastime
Giving folk feelings divine
In thy heart a joyous wealth
For everyone on Earth
Nothing can surpass poetry
The poet writes in ecstasy
Giving folk inspiration
Expressing a world of creation

Words giving folk charm
Their heart and mind calm
Into life some meaning
A venture of good feeling
World of creation be wonderfully relaxing
To the heart diligent and soothing
Folk visualise poetry expressed
Reflects with lives and feel impressed

Power of the pen is welcomed
As hearts and soul doth blend
By words of courage and hope
Around the world inspiring folk
Perusing poetry from the start
Graciously gives folk a spark
Filling their soul with extreme passion
In a world of creation

In changing times of today
Folk charmed in many ways
Enhance poetry admired
Throughout the world desired
Every living soul has problems

Inspiring poetry releases them
Reaching out thy soul to open
A world of creation by the pen.

Josephine Foreman

Bless 'Em All

They risked their lives and their limbs
Throughout the wars
Their bravery was all that they knew.
They fought for our futures
Through battles that roared
And were awarded posthumously too.

They defended their country
Against all that was hurled
The choice was not theirs to choose
They gave their all for this modern world
Not able to express their views.

They never stopped to question why
Such conflicts called their names
No explanations as to why they died
Or why they came home lame.

For they were there and trained to fight
To fend off all the foe
Many, alas, never saw peace light
But were awarded posthumously though.

Now on stalls on war-free grounds
Be on markets or on car boot
They are selling those lives for a couple of pounds
Just to pin on someone's suit.

Peter T Ridgway

'Life' (Of Profoundness)

Sunrise is the first dawn of day:
Light, life and hope;
Sunset is the second dawn of day,
The twilight of dark night - the owl's time,
Where all is on hold in ignorant repose;
Clutch at the day, for:
The days become less,
And all too soon, twilight will pose,
Then eternal darkness will impose and - prevail;
Follow the sun and it will never set.

Still cooling, the planet Earth is slowly shrinking;
Volcanoes - simmer; storms - build;
Clocks - tick, ring and chime;

Time - ticks on:

The first dawn -

When the clouds are light and wispy,
The sky - so blue! In relief,
The soft, pastel moon becomes a crescent ghost when
From eastern folds, the bright, western sun
Slowly emerges, bringing an iridescent, spiderweb dawn,
That serenely surrounds and stirs the balsams of the woods,
And peaceful, dreamland hollows,

There is a strange silence,
An intense and broody stillness,
A calm before an unknown drama -
A drama full of expectancy;

Graceful, timid deer scent the uncanny air
And roam with nervous step;

Time - ticks on:

It is the strutting cock herald's time of day - the time when
Cuckoo spit whitely froths,
Evening primroses flop asleep, but
The beautiful morning glories trumpets unfold,
And the sunflowers beam -
At season's time;

Time - ticks on:

It is light:

Dew bead droplets crystal hang -
From the branches of gnarled trees,
Gather and drip from casement window sills
                              And guttered eaves;
Descending roots are deeply drinking,
Waking plants unfurl their fronds and leaves,
And stirring flowers reveal fresh petal blooms
With anthers full of fragrant, rich pollen;
                Insects - murmur,
                Aphids - suckle,
                Wombs - stir;
To the rustle of leaves,
Birds embrace the building day,
With sweet call;
Slugs and snails crawl and slither,
Their crisscross trails glisten;
Rodents scurry and hide; stag beetles -
Land on their backs;

                                        Time - ticks on:

It is breakfast time:

Dawn spiderwebs of woven, delicate weave
Entrap unmindful prey;
Infant children stretch awake, then cry
For the maternal, latescent teat of flowing,
Sweet, nutritiousness, tiny fists fold, clench, then,
Gently pummel;
The owl has flown;
                'It is Life;'   Time - ticks on:

The sun ascends, inching ever brighter
To spur diurnal life:
                                        Time - ticks on:
The sky lightens, and pure, spreading light
Floods the dales and clears the early mists from peaks, and
                        down-land hills, valleys - softly emerge;
Sunrays course through forest glades, copse and spinney;
Squirrels sway the branches of the trees;

Pools and millponds ripple and sparkle;
Streams of crystal water stream through dapple woodlands green;
Frogs' spawn - at season's time:

In warming orchards of budding fruitfulness,
Busy honeybees hum, then reap the fragrant pollen
And sow the seeds; honey sweetens;
Wheat and corn grow; blackberries swell with sugared blackness -
                                        at season's time;

Flies buzz! and on pasture fields of green,
In leafy bowers and paddocks chained,
Horse and cattle graze and steam, their tails flick;
Sheep, goats and offspring bleat -
There is a faint tinkle of bells -
A farmer's dog crawls low;
Rabbits hop over burrowed grass and spiky, gorse-tough land; preying birds hover;

                        Time - ticks on:

Light, warm breezes wave the watered rushes
And bend the tips of the tall, lean rye;
Seas swell, roll and recede -
Dragging a dredged, seaweed drenched shore, where hangs
                        a strong smell of fresh brine;
Whirling gulls give vent to yelping cries;
Rivers flow, fish swim, shellfish bask;
Crabs crawl-awkwardly amongst rocky, muddy pebble beds;

Somewhere, in primitive corners of outer continents,
Native women draw the water holes; the sludge disturbed,
Breakfast pots are set to bubble - on spiralling brushwood fires;
Cur dogs bark, whine and snarl! Beasts of prey stalk;
                        Snakes glide - ready to strike;
In drifting deserts, where hot, storm winds blow, camels chew the
                        cud and sail the dunes and waves of drifted sand;
Pyramids erode; date palms quench on oasis water;
Scorpions are braced to sting!

                        Time - ticks on:

All around, many relentless walking feet pound the footway clay beneath,
As commerce begins and the harsh wheels of cacophonous industry
                        squeal and ring;

                        Time - ticks on: until, sunset - the
second dawn descends,
                and darkness - soon to prevail.

William G Thomas

Strangers Are Friends

A shaft of light escapes,
From above the curtains.
The gate shudders,
The wind bitterly cold -
With each advancing step.

A knock, ring, smile -
That ever practised phrase.
Gosh, is that the time?
No, no, must go -
Another time, perhaps.

The path seems longer
Walking back.
Another five to go.
The light is fading fast
And tomorrow will not do.

A knock, ring, smile -
Come in of course
Enveloped in warmth
A welcome stranger.

This greeting is real,
A cup of tea, a chat
Escape for a few minutes
From the evil wind.

Then back on the road.
A shiver, a shake.
The interviewer goes on -
A lonely figure against
A black blanket.

Yes,
With encouragement
And a smile with warmth
They are real people.

But do you ever take time
To notice them?

Louise Weatherby

The Charioteer

With battle colours flying
He went into the fray
With strong and faithful courage
He faced the dreadful day

The hours of tortuous training
With fortitude were borne;
The nervous apprehension
On many a fearful morn

Had now come to fruition,
Upon him soon were cast
The awful unknown terrors
To bravely face at last

With great determination
His trusty sword beside
The battleground awaiting
He forward made his stride

What clash and roar and screeching!
What cacophony of sound!
The twisting and the turning
And the clamour all around!

His jangled nerves were straining,
He quelled his rising fear,
He held his weapon firmly,
This faithful charioteer

And forward ever forward
The obstacles o'ercome
He slew his foes to right and left
Until the deeds were done!

Then slowly and more slowly
His day's warfaring won
He brought his warhorse safely back
A warrior craving home

With praises heaped around his neck
With laurels closely wreathed
The hero proudly holds his head
His shining sword now sheathed

Then climbing forth, his eyes alight
A soldier, done his best!
A heart now bursting with delight!
Dear Laurie's passed his test!

Barbara Jean Settle

Twice As Modern

After the Germans won the second World War
A new order emerged.
People didn't just do as they wanted,
They did what others wanted.
After mopping up the last few pockets of resistance,
Attention turned to scientific advancement.
A major breakthrough in this area
Was the invention of 'Time Kite'.
Bringing with it the possibility of great benefits
To the victors worldwide.
Fourteen specially chosen 'Healthites'
(Thirteen men and one woman named Mary)
Were about to go back in time, two thousand years.
The result of which would invent God
And lose them the second World War
And see the rise of mass migration and a third World War.
A best selling book records their adventures
As time travellers,
From the turning of water to wine,
To the restoring of sight to the blind.
Not to mention the feeding of five thousand
With a food replicator appliance.
They never came back,
But the future changed in ways
No one could have imagined.
It was as if they scored an own goal so to speak.

Vann Scytere

Eco-Dream State

From the very nightmare of my fear
With the indelible crust of prehistoric message
Out of the island cliff caves
Around painted, broken spears
Contrasts with the dream of gorse yellow
And wintered, cracked paths
With the water dancing shoreline to rhythm and blues
They screamed to chase the auto-geometric
Tightening of the territories
His sci-fi ideas made the northern wind turn to ice
Now above the seasonal DNA
Will we pick up the fragrance of dust-wrapped home
Stifle the unnatural forest fire
Come face to face with thoughts galactic compass
And clear every crazed move for the smile of flowers
Then amaze ourselves with the over-gilding truth.

Edward Tanguy

The Price Of War

She started running a tear in her eye
Bombs were dropping burning buildings light the sky,
Where could she shelter? Where could she go?
Would she make it to the cellar door?
She ran so fast she thought her heart would stop
The noise of the bombs made her ears go pop,
Then a searing pain hit her across her back
She stumbled and fell, then all went black.
A man nearby who had seen it all
Rushed to catch her and break her fall.
He picked her up, blood poured from her back
Her breathing was shallow, her body went slack.
She lay limp in his arms but nothing was said
She was only ten and now she was dead.

Myrddin Jones

Land Of My Birth

England is a beauteous place
Full of wonder, full of grace.
When I stand on distant shores
She calls me back to her once more.

The sea of so many hues
Dark grey-green to misty blues
Laps shores off all her coasts
From Lands End to John O'Groats.

Many places can be found where
There is no other sound
Save cry of wild fowl in flight
And hoot of owl at dead of night.

Come take me by the hand
Into this enchanted land.
In an English country lane
You find the violets bloom again.

O'er misty moors and craggy heights
For travellers' sweet delight.
A room in an English inn
And many a tale there to spin.

Now all in England is not fair
For industry does taint the air.
Where without it would we be
Fair island in the middle of the sea.

When I wander, when I roam
My heart is never far from home.
For there is no place on Earth
Like England, land of my birth.

Joyce Brown

Don't Ever Leave Me

Don't ever leave me
It would break my heart
I've always loved you
Right from the start

We had a lot of good times
As time went by
And if you ever left me
I think I would die

At night I dream of you
That you are in my arms
I don't want to wake up
And miss all your charms

So darling, don't leave me
My love for you is true
And should we be parted
You'd leave me oh so blue.

R Boyd

Country Girl

Roses in profusion
Blossom anew
Daffodil, crocus
Flowers of every hue
Hollyhock and bluebell
Lush meadows green
Cherry trees drenched in colour
Mother Nature's yearly scene.

Soon a smiling lass appears
On this fragrant morn
Eyes of blue, hair as waving corn
Singing softly she goes on her way
The country girl
Whose beauty
Enhanced a perfect day.

Chris Stacey

Life Is Not What It Seems

Through the passing of the years,
I've had my share of sorrow,
And shed a few tears.

I've experienced love, and a little hate,
Yet still I leave my path to God and to fate.

I look into the mirror,
Through eighteen year old eyes,
An old man stares back at me,
Showing my demise.

Life is what you make it,
Embrace it with all your might,
Cherish those special moments,
They are your guiding lights.

Memories fade with age,
We struggle to remember,
Like a roaring fire dying,
We leave a burning ember.

And now it's time to say farewell,
And share our families' love,
To justify our time on Earth,
To the Lord up above.

Ray Brown

Open A New Leaf

All disabilities: right straightened now.
I feel like a leaf, green and unfurling.
The stars are chortling, not at but with me.
It is not autumn. I could be sprung out.
I am feeling like I am above my wheelchair.

Barry Welburn

The Root Of The Problem

There are many problems to be solved in this life
We search for the answers sometimes in vain
Prayers are said, tears are shed in its train
Think deeply and sincerely, don't continue in strife
For the root of the problem is embedded in your heart.

Think of a tree planted deep in soil
You wait for days, months and years for it to produce
The fruit you long for, bites you can induce
Be patient my dear, never tire in your toil
For you have planted, you have watered a tree of hope.

The tree of hope has problems in its roots
To solve it you must have faith to dig into it
For you wrestle and sweat until you see a pit
Be careful when you see the soil sinking beneath your foot
For then the problem is shifting straight up its branches.

At this point, my friend, you must search your heart
To trace what the problem is and from where it derives
As the root has moved to your heart and there it thrives
Disperse the problem now with faith lest the devil will start
To turn your life, just as a tree, upside down.

Rebecca Williams

Plop, Plop, Plop

Just listen to that rain!
Oh no, it's those pesky seagulls again,
Swooping and pooping, flying low,
Making a mess wherever they go.
Why can't they leave us alone for a day,
Return to the sea, far, far away?
Cleaning up after them is not much fun,
There's much better things to do in the sun.

Mara Wellman

The Weeping Valleys

The valleys and the hills will always meet
Those hedgerow pathways have become concrete streets
The farmyard barns have been replaced by supermarket shops
Those pretty farm cottages become large bus station with glass-like stops

The tiny brooks have been covered over where once the children played
Their swimming place that once filled with merriment
Is sadly taken away
There were once sweet pastures here but now litter fills the streets
Those vile plastic bags and chip boxes are now under our feet

They build their large airports, their planes like stars fill the skies
That stream of carbon gases that float like clouds as they fly
Those speeding cars and heavy traffic spews out their deadly load
When those speeding drivers are the biggest danger upon those gas-filled roads

Those beautiful pasture lands have been badly damaged for years
Those fine trees in the forest with those acid rain-like tears
There will be broken glass and discarded tins dumped in a stream
You will hear the cries of the moorlands and wounded ground will scream.

J F Grainger

Religions

Rumours spread, which the godly person may wisely dispel
About devout maniacs, whose strangely warped minds
Adhere to strange beliefs of unholy and curious kinds.
Such sects decry our 'Regal Society of the British Infidel'.
Members are drawn solely from the drinking classes
Whose numbers have been greatly reduced one hears
By the criminally high tax levied upon English beers.
Most wise infidels drink out of pint pot glasses,
Are part educated, and often have heard it said
'Forfeit nowadays is the life of the unbeliever
Even now in the hands of the Official Receiver'.
Some maniacs may such infidels gladly behead.
Little remains for this thoughtful philosopher to say,
Save, 'Last orders, drink up. Amen, and lettuce pray.'

Anne Omnibus

Peace All Over The World

No more fighting, no more killing,
No more destruction of brutal wars,
No more innocent people left dying,
Screaming and crying on the cold floors.

No more guns, no more weapons,
Please stop them being made,
Round a table discussing alternatives
For us all to have better days.

Scattering love, warmth and kindness,
Like the sunshine and gentle rain,
All running free in the wild wind,
Singing and laughing with
Your loved ones and friends.

We should all stand tall like the highest mountains,
Protecting the honour to be here in this world.
We should be holding hands together
Watching the peace and the love dove birds.

Maddie Reade

School Holidays

'You should be outside at play,'
Said Grandma wanting some peace.
'You've been stuck in this house all day,
Now I want your antics to cease.'

'But you won't let us play in the rain
And there's no Internet access about,
So we tease you by groaning in pain
Whilst giving each other a clout.'

'Well, next year I'm going to France,
Solo - without you kids, or your mother,
And as I view chateaux - perchance
Someone else will be plagued with your pother.'

Judith Roberts

Sunkissed Morning Dew

Early morning dew on grass catching sun rays
Glistening like crystal drops, the most glorious of days
Spiders busy overnight,
Webs woven, covered in dew, a wondrous sight

Cattle resting with the calves in morning mist
Silhouette-like,
Birdsong sweet amid the trees
A gentle rustle of the leaves

Grasshoppers moving, easily seen
Between blades of grass, a darker green
Through overhead branches, sunbeams filter down
Creating pools of gold upon the ground

A fairy tale, a wonderland,
Nature's beauty, created by God's hand.

Gertrude Schoën

My Father And Me

The love between my father and me
Was very plain for all to see
We helped each other to the end
As he was more than a father, he was my best friend
I am so sad since he has died
I can't get over it, so hard I have tried
With each and every passing day
The hurt just will not go away
People say that time will heal
But that's just not the way I feel
So now each day to God I pray
To ease my pain in His own way
Then I'll be able to get on with my life
Rid of all the turmoil and strife
And once again my life will be
As it always was, so very happy.

Deirdre Rawlinson

Our Summer Holiday

The holiday gladly awaited
Had surely come at last,
Two weeks of frolicking and fun
And hoping we'd have lots of sun.

The sun was shining brightly
As we started out from home,
The children were all excited
By the pleasures that would come.

The journey was a nightmare
As south the traffic roared,
We were very late arriving
But food was soon prepared.

Once the car was emptied
They all raced to the beach,
With buckets and spades and bathing things
The sea was soon within our reach.

One day we visited a local farm
Saw cows and sheep and chickens
We all helped to collect the eggs
Unfortunately, dropping some to smithers.

Another day we went to a fair
With roundabouts and swings,
Waltzers and the bumper cars
And many other things.

We said we'd had a wonderful time
And made many new friends,
So we'll look forward to next year
And our summer holiday again.

Caroline Russell

Fireflies

Like starstruck fireflies we dance in the summer skies.
Frantic weaving, twisting, turning,
Reaching out, our bodies yearning.
A passionate embrace, two lovers face to face.

Honey dripping from my lips
As we are locked with interlacing hips
That speed like runaway trains
Lust coursing through our veins
As you send me soaring again, again . . . and again.

Pleasure ripples through my limbs,
Such delight from the touch of your skin.
Fulfilled and fulfilling, passions are soothing.
Slowly now our forms are moving,
Shallow breathing, rise and fall, as daylight calls.

Sarah Whatley

The Fisherman And His Net

Sat in a little room at the top of the winding stairs
Overlooking the grey North Sea
And enjoying it and all its guises
With dextrous fingers although arthritic
Possessing skill beyond compare.
The old fisherman mends his net with loving care.
Fingers working at a furious rate
Weaving the net at his feet
Many a fish have they caught
Silver darlings of the briny deep
Many memories of a lifetime at sea
Boats and men expensively bought.
All through the house swirls the aroma of his trade
Tar of the nets and rumours of fish
Wind blown through gaps in the glass
Bringing news of the salty ways.

Andrew P McIntyre

The Lonesome Hero

I saw him sitting in the street,
He had no shoes, he had no feet.
'Buy a poppy,' you will hear him say,
'I haven't sold many today.
The Legion are very good,
They give me shelter, they give me food,
I sell the poppies so I can say
I'm helping to pay my way.
I'm alive, my mates are dead,
Your poppy will give one family bread.
The widows and orphans they suffered too,
We were scared and so afraid,
At our posts we stayed;
We fought till we could fight no more,
Then made our way to Dunkirk shore.
We were bombed and shelled both night and day,
Then we finally got away.
We were rescued by a motley crew,
We were many, they were few.
Please buy a poppy, lady, do,
I only have just a few.'
I gave the money I had got,
He thanked me, gave me the lot.
'God bless you, Missus,' he did say,
I watched him wheel himself away.
He disappeared into the night,
I watched till he was out of sight.
Thanks to him I have another day,
He fought for us so we could be free;
He'll be alright with the Legion and we.

C W Groves

The Modern World - Dinosaur Viewpoint

'Hello, can you hear me? I'm in the airport . . .'
We can *all* hear you, should be my retort.
Mobile phones maybe a mirror of the age,
But to some, like me, they can create rage.
They're OK for business, arranging a meet . . .
Why not talk *quietly* - that would be neat.
Even young kids with their make-up and bling,
Cannot last five minutes without giving a ring
To their friend down the street who's in line of sight,
Everyone phoning by day and by night.
No one listens, they all have to shout,
What's wrong with a text - too quiet I doubt!
Laptops seem to be the thing to carry,
In hand or on shoulder by the owner they marry.
They've replaced the car to a certain extent,
By their users' auras of wealth and good intent.
As for me, I'm retired and grey,
I've done my thing and had my day.
Technology bores me, but I keep my peace,
I don't use computers or iPod sales increase.
The Royal Mail service still carries my notes,
It may be slow, but has all my votes.
Possibly, I do yearn for times in the past,
When manners not 'me' was the thing meant to last.
Everything now is geared to speed,
It's got to be instant because of the need.
Why not slow down the pace of our life,
And live a bit longer with much less strife?
If the National Grid fails and electronics all crash,
Would this be the time for 'Bluetooth' to gnash?
The yuppies of today will completely be lost,
Without their gadgets to work out the cost.
The likes of myself will continue to amble
Through life as we see it without all the scramble.

Alan R Coughlin

A Broken Soul

I have a broken soul
Which I cannot mend,
Its edges are worn and pitted
From what it has had to defend.
I have a broken soul
It's so frayed it will not seal,
I have a broken soul
That will not seem to heal.

My spirit that kept me strong
Has gone beyond my grasp,
Now it is a wisp of smoke
Like a candle blown,
Drifting away through my past
And leaving me all alone.

My mind is misshapen
But a secret it must stay
Because people lack understanding
And they keep me at bay,
So the truth remains hidden
Behind a cheerful smile,
My mind is so black and sad
But they only want the smile.

I once had some hope
But it's smouldering now
Beneath the rockfall
Of thoughts most foul.
But I can see a glimmer of light
It glows so dimly, but never goes out
Occasionally it flares and shines bright
But there's always someone there
Who will put it out.

I get exhausted with trying my best
So I hide in bed and give it a rest
But hope, it often keeps flaring
Giving me no peace,
So I will keep trying when

I have rested my mind
And hope the people out there
Will be tolerant and kind.

Lynda Wilkins

The River Tyne

I start my journey in the hills, a small and sparkling flow,
Bubbling along heather and gorse, down to the valley below.
Passing fields on either side where farmers sow and reap,
Where cows lie down when hard rain falls side by side with sheep.
I gently flow through Hexham, a very old market town,
Where the tower of the abbey is always looking down.
Humpback bridges, stepping stones all from long ago,
To help the people on their way, built, I do not know.
Now the scene is changing, past Dunston, I wend my way,
No more the keel men and their coal, the stathes lie still today.
I'm winding down to Gateshead, I think I can smell the sea,
The river is much cleaner now, was that a fish passed me?
Ranks flour mill, the Baltic is now an art gallery,
The sage is a music centre all gloss and shining to see.
The old parish church of St Mary's, small but the oldest there,
A visitors' centre it has become, no more does it hear a prayer.
Newcastle on the other side, new law courts I can see,
The quayside market where they sell their wares,
Much smaller than it used to be.
I'm passing the ferries and tug boats, under the bridges at speed,
Seven they say there are, I'm sure that's more than they need.
The seabirds are flying overhead, I'm nearing my journey's end,
For the lighthouse and piers at Tynemouth and Shields
Have become my oldest friends,
Into the cold North Sea I flow, and tomorrow I start again.

Mary Smiles

Courage

'Help me, please help me,'
He heard a voice say.
It was after the fighting
On that well known day.

The offensive was beaten
And now the retreat
With the gasping and panting
And pounding of feet.

Somehow he slowed
From his mad, headlong flight,
A wounded soldier lay there,
Left for dead in the fight.

There he stood, his legs shaking,
Turned aside from the race
And he noticed the yearning
On the other man's face.

He thought of the trenches
Offering safety quite near
And he thought of the firing
Which he could still hear.

He thought of his family
And struggled to choose
He was young, strong and active
With so much to lose.

And the shells were still bursting
And the guns firing too
As in that split second
He knew what to do.

So he helped up his comrade
And slowly they came
Yes, slowly they stumbled
From that field of ill-fame.

And the guns went on firing
And the shells shed their light
On the mud and the dead men
Until next morning's light.

A new day has started
Its horror and pain
And a young man is wondering:
Could I do that again?

Mary Joyce Le Vicount

Is There An Answer?

As we sit here watching the telly
The news gets worse and worse
Stabbings and shootings, fights on our streets
Can anything now get worse?

Oh yes, indeed it can
A photo appears of a handsome young man
Somebody's son, husband, brother or dad
Has this country gone totally mad?

Our finest young ladies, our finest young men
Volunteer to protect us from evil, but then
These brave young people are sent far and wide
And then we hear how some have died.

As we watch the telly, another photo appears
Another family reduced to tears
Whilst most of the men and women here
Also hold these lives so very dear.

With pride and respect we watch with dismay
Another body flown home today
What can we do? What can we say?
In desperation we can only pray.

P Burton-Westcott

Wishful Thinking

Many folks wish they'd done this and that in life
Been like the rich and famous, born under a lucky star
Had the breaks to come when they most needed
Or even the simple hopes that things kept on par

Wished to keep on even keel, so says one phrase
Live an uncomplicated life, or have a dream come true
That windfall many want, for most a hope forlorn
But they will gamble, hoping they're ahead in the queue

Wish one had the push and shove of such as they
Or indeed the talent somehow that brings that success
That elevates them on to those high echelons
A tenacious few in life who'll not settle for less

As one gets older and needs lessen, dreams forgotten
That one chance of Lady Luck smiling on us remains
Hope springs eternal, we put faith in its charity and gamble
On some lottery or pools win or Premium Bond gains

If one's taken what seems a stony road could with hindsight
Put back the clock and be more assertive than in the past
Alas, if we're all puppets of some higher deity's creation
Pulling the strings, we just humble members of the cast

A simple cog in this universe but an earthly creation
Programmed to be whom or what we are when born
A standard rose or super bloom on the tree of life
Or just an also ran like the common old garden thorn

Many born crippled for life that can be also short
No sweetness such as even a most humble thorn may known
May live an average span of life with chronic ailments
So one should wish them their suffering were not so

We may wish in our own lesser traumas we'd been patient
When stresses and strains of life had got us down
Not snarled, turned the other cheek, had that patience
Which sets some apart from others, a halo their crown

If one had a magic wand to wave at times not indiscriminately
More a healing type with no Midas-like gold touch
But could cure the illnesses of those we hold dear who suffer
Worth more than riches could bring, for they'd be nonesuch

The healing power of say Lourdes or other place folk go
Grasping their faith albeit so many times it seems in vain
Miracles though few are still known to happen somewhere
But like the rest of life it's only a chosen few can gain

Like having five loaves and two fishes to feed a multitude
Or an aircraft dropping supplies to a starving throng
It's only they who are the strongest get a lion's share
What a wonderful world, said Louis Armstrong in his song
Oh Yeah.

Philip Temperton

A Change?

Do we know where we are in time in this world?
Have we travelled the paths that we should?
As we gaze ahead at whatever may be
We fight to move from the places we stood.

Is there hope, is there change?
Will hearts freely care?
Will the thoughts in our minds
Speak with voices that share?

Is there the strength within us to change?
To forgive, to comfort, to care?
And do we truly have the faith
To remove what shouldn't be there?

Look at now and wonder
If one step can become a day.
And with strength of faith, we strive for good
That makes evil fade away.

Pauline Foster

Motherhood

Motherhood is
All embracing, self effacing,
Maturing, enduring,
Ever growing in the knowing
Of the child.

Motherhood is
Fun and laughter that comes after
Frustration's tears and night-time fears.
It's years of worrying, always hurrying
On through life.

Motherhood is
Loving and caring, never despairing;
A tug at the heart that won't depart,
An intangible, infrangible
Meaning to life.

Jean M White

The Fast Lane

I always found the fast lane
Tiring. Now, being retired,
I don't have to work, or even look
For work. I can take my time
Getting up, and listen to music all day.
There's not much to do, although
There are still bills to pay.
I can read and write and paint,
And do a little housework.
But it doesn't matter
If I shirk.

Keith Murdoch

Red Rose

My love is like a red, red rose
It's so beautiful to see
My love is like a red, red rose
It grows for you and me

My love is like a red, red rose
Its perfume smells so sweet
My love is like a red, red rose
It's so beautiful and neat

My love is like a red, red rose
When the sun shines so bright
My love is like a red, red rose
It goes to sleep at night.

Marion Paton

Smiles

We all have the ability to smile
A precious gift which costs us nothing
Use as many as you like
Because they never diminish.

There are all kinds of smiles
Joy from the birth of a baby
And smiles turning to laughter, so smile
At strangers and receive smiles in return.

A smile cannot be bought or sold
They are freely given
They cannot be lost or stolen
But destroyed by a frown.

A smile is like a ray of sunshine,
Beaming and spreading across the face.
Besides it takes more muscles
To frown than to smile. So smile.

Vera Entwistle

Permanence?

When someone dies, what happens to their memories?
They were recollectable yesterday
Part of the mindsets that make up
The universe.
How can they not exist today
When so widely gleaned
Just because one single creature has ceased to be?

When someone dies, what happens to their knowledge?
It was communicable yesterday
Part of the intelligence that fuels
The universe.
How can it not exist today
When so uniquely gathered in
Just because one single creature has ceased to be?

When someone dies, what happens to their experience?
It was demonstrable yesterday
Extensively accumulated from everything that made up
Their universe.
How can it not exist today
When gained from myriad others
Whose lives go on?Just its storehouse that has ceased to be.

When someone dies, can God recycle these good attributes
That were there yesterday?
Part of our total world which we accord as in
God's universe.
What can He do with them
So rich in great diversity
With power to well-inform a world - where just one has ceased to be?

Neil Inkley

Ever Thine

My most precious, precious love -
I hear you calling me
Through a chillingly cold night -
I hear you beloved.

I want to reach out to you -
Cool your fevered brow -
Quench your thirst
And feed your nightly hunger.

Fight on - beloved
I will hear your voice -
Even a million miles away.
I am yours - until the end of time.

Two lost souls -
Thrown to the waves on a tempestuous
Sea of life.
Yet love conquers
All suffering -
Heals all ills.

Fight on beloved -
I hear you calling me.
As time stand still -

For all those
    Who *love*.

Nina Graham

Agony Of Heart

Mother, why so much
fury in these storms from you
since the last one penetrated
into the rock face of my heart

I surrender to the storm
and I'm scarred again and again
desperate, grasping
for stability in tablets
for the strength to breathe
for life . . .

Doctors tell me to
desert this weather cycle round you
relocate my expectancy to an empty place,
give up family life
and
deal with the pain of need instead . . .

Abigail Markey

The Garden Of Dreams

Dare to dream the impossible dream!
Let your thoughts flow - free as a stream;
For dreams are seeds planted in the mind
With repetitive thought the roots of which find
A place to take hold in a fertile bed
Of creative ideas inside the head
Watered with visualisation - new buds appear
And fed with faith - there's nothing to fear
Because detailed pictures are essential to nourish
The blooms of success which are bound to flourish
With constant attention to the 'eye of the mind'
We see dreams take shape and reality find!

Trish Andow

This Blissful Moment

Nature is all around wherever you are
So let it teach you its hidden secrets
Its secrets of peacefulness and silence
That envelops its surroundings.

See how deeply at peace it is
There is that sensuousness of serenity and calmness
That prevails around it
So be aware of its emanation of stillness and peace.

And notice how still and deeply rooted it is
For nature holds you in its embrace
Cloaking your whole mind and body
You and nature need one another.

Now let your mind be aware of its beauty
And connect with it at a deeper level
Allow it to be your teacher
Teaching you its stillness.

The mind goes deeper and beyond the physical body
And is now still and calm in nature's arm
With silence surrounding me
How do I describe further this blissful moment?

Michael Curry

Teardrops

In my attic I found a dusty old frame
The picture inside a young girl with no name,
The artist had painted teardrops on her face
This picture was left in the dark attic's space.

I took it downstairs and I looked at each wall
I wanted the sunniest wall of them all.
The one by the window, the sun shone all day long
Now she smiles down at me and her teardrops have gone.

Leslie Hogarth

Untitled

What makes a nation fall so far,
That all its values fail, that all
Its people lose their way and

Follow leaders, forcing them
To torture and to kill, making
Murderers of children, who
Smile, inflicting pain,

For false ideas and principles,
Against all normal human feelings
And, all to no avail, for all to end
In misery and only bones remain.

The land, become a charnel house,
That, once, was thought a garden,
With millions of photographs of
The murdered dead displayed?

And yet, despite the massacres,
Green shoots appear, in blood-
Soaked mud, the mass graves
Of the slain and, smiles upon
Survivors' faces, as nature
And humanity, re-focus
And prevail.

Yet, always there's
The question:

Could it occur again?

R A Garside

North Kessock

I'm sitting in my garden
Looking out to sea,
The sun beams on the ripples,
A striking sight to see.

Four swans glide on the water
In a little inlet bay,
Their stately heads all held aloft,
They brighten up my day.

Small birds flit from bush to bush,
Ducks dabble on the shore,
This indeed is heaven-sent,
Who could ask for more?

The Kessock Bridge looks splendid
Taking traffic speedily by.
The sun glints off car windows
Flashing mirrors to the sky.

Some pleasure boats moored in the Firth
Command a stately scene,
With cameras clicking constantly
To capture views on screen.

Ah, now I see a great big splash
Break up the silver tide,
The dolphins at aerobics,
Across the other side.

Oh, Kessock's such a pretty place,
Of that there is no doubt,
Its attractions are alluring,
A host to shout about.

Violet Beattie

Won Now

The end is the end of now
But the start of a new beginning.
As spring brings us new life
Death cancels all that's tired
And all that's tried and weary.

Life's a race that's never won
Till death's our final trophy.

Think not of death as losing
But just the end for now.
Loved ones not lost eternally
But one's last breath - like spring -
Awakens painted summer skies
Brushed by an angel's wing.

Though lease of life has ended
Each end's a new beginning
And when the race, for now, is lost
In essence this means winning.

If death's that final trophy
That shining, guiding light
Don't mourn for 'now'
But embrace 'evermore' -
And at last glimpse God's goodness and might.

Nadia Nuth

Baby Harry

'Lo, children are a heritage of the Lord' (Ps 127 v3)
The scriptures clearly declare
And we believe God's precious word
For the child now in our care.

We prayed for the embryo in the womb
As the babe grew day by day
And now plead for wisdom, guidance and strength
To teach him the truth, the way.

What name shall we give this little one?
A boy growing up bold and brave
Serving the Master all his days
Who died his soul to save.

O Harry, may you know *the* faith
That resists temptation's snares
And Christ becomes your all in all
To disperse all doubts and fears

Our darling baby, we'll pray for you
And love you with all our hearts
For you came to us from the Lord himself
Who united two sweethearts.

Doreen Reeves

Captain Cook

In your absence
I have an excuse to invent you.
To scratch your name
into a toilet wall with a penknife.
Invent you piece by piece
to make my invention whole.
Construct each intestine
to the right length.
Carve your skull
from poems
rattling around my head
in those early morning dawns
when you're not around
and I lie in bed
imagining what you look like when you're dreaming.

Sophie Tomlinson

Secrets Of Stonehenge

I dreamt of Stonehenge and had to go there
For I needed my soul to be laid bare.

I asked a question. Was he for me?
Only the stones could see, but would they reveal the answer to me?

Deep down in my heart I know he belongs to another.
Even though if I had the chance I would be his lover.

I could feel the energy radiate from the stones,
Right through every part of my being to my bones.

They tell me I need to be brave,
For the peace in my spirit which I crave.

Carol Brown

How Do I Look?

'How do I look?'
I asked my friend
As I showed her my brand new dress
She said, 'It's far too tight and much too bright
I'm really not impressed.'

'How do I look?'
I asked her again
As I modelled a cropped top and slacks
She said, 'You can't wear that, it makes you look fat
I think you should take them back.'

'How do I look?'
I asked my sister
As I teetered in high-heeled shoes
She said, 'The colour's not right, they look far too tight
They'd look better on me than on you.'

'How do I look?'
I asked my dad
Feeling proud in my new party gear
He said, 'I don't like what you're wearing, it's much too daring
Folk will think you're a hussy, I fear.'

'How do I look?'
I asked my mum
Giving a twirl in my smart tailored suit
Taking my hand, she said, 'You look grand
Whatever you wear you look cute.'

This just goes to prove
When all's said and done
If you want the truth, ask your mum.

Freda Pilton

Our Historic Town

Glitter of waves and ripple of water
Bid our hearts rejoice and recall with pride
Our seafaring forebears who from this town
Set sail at dawn, going out with the tide.
Raising of anchors and furling of sails
Rigging of schooners with long lissom hull
Brings thoughts of sailors in cabin below
While skies are riven with cry of seagull.
Fronds of cool seaweed, green and amber-brown,
Sudden eddies of spray over hidden rocks
And the ships under topsail thrashing by,
Wind in the rigging and creaking of blocks.
We sing now the praise of men of the sea
Who toil on the deep for you and for me.

Caroline Buddery

Is The Veil Lifted?

I sit alone
In the depth of the night
In the depth of the universe
In the awesome cosmos
Amidst the deafening silence
Of the stars
And before me
Sits the truth
The only truth
The everlasting truth
And is the veil lifted?
And can I see?

David Stephen Marshall

Yorkshire Heritage

I dream of nineteen seventy-two
The three-day week and miners' woes
Although those memories are too few
And love and life erase go-slows

Those Yorkshire ghosts
They linger . . . linger

Funny how that tragedy
Set in train a fearful journey
Embarkation/transportation
Like some 19th century foray

Where Yorkshire ghosts
They slumber . . . slumber

Moorland hill and urban chaos
Swapped for New World's barren splendour
Ullaru's brooding menace
Like a spoil heap's great surrender

To Yorkshire ghosts
Who slumber . . . slumber?

Still we hold that sharpened fragment
Though the landscape changes round us
Sleek new structures, empty towers
Like the pit wheel o'er us glowers

Waking Yorkshire ghosts
Who slumbered . . . slumbered

Streams and moors and heath surround us
This our heritage, stamped on pavements
Let us have these memories ground us
As we steer our future movements

Resurrecting Yorkshire ghosts
Who find us . . . bind us

Portia Pennington

Who Am I?

A wife
A mother
A daughter
A sister
A friend

I am here but do you need me
Or are you in turmoil with your emotions?
Sometimes we are one
My body aches to make it right for you
But what I want for you, is it your wish?
I cannot fulfil what you want now
Though I am here should you still need me
We are so close but miles apart
One day perhaps we'll be as one.
I am here should you need me, I know you are there
Some day I will tell you what your friendship has meant
But then you know!
My heart aches with my emotions, I love
You all in different ways
But how can I get through to you
Divide myself for all of you
Where do I stand?
Suffice to say I love you all.

Eileen McCulloch

Walk Beside

I love your self-confidence
And your insecurity

I love your drive and energy
And your isolation

I love your depth and cool insight
The lightness of your humour

I love your skin and all that's within
I'm proud to walk beside you

I love your boy and also your man
The tenderness that they have shown me

I love your thoughts and words and deeds
And the world you are creating

I love your head, your heart and soul
The weave of past and future

I love your love and joy and pain
Your culture always around you

I love the struggle that defines your life
And ache for you to find peace

I love your sighs and your silences
The tears that hide in your eyes

I love how you dare to be open with me
I treasure the words that you say

I love your love, your fire, your truth
I love to know you

You said to me, 'I adore you'
My heart is full for you

Sigrid Fisher

Drink Of This

It ran before me
A river of red
Warm and slick its waters were
I cupped my hands and drank deeply
It tasted of copper and passion
It tasted of life
And of death
I drank until I could drink no more

Over my tongue that richness trickled
Then down my gullet
Slipping its way down that gulping passage
Thick and creamy it wound its way

Heat warmed my chest
And then bloomed in my belly

All the parts of me knew that heat
Like wildfire it raced through my limbs
Down to the very tips of my toes
And the ends of my grasping fingers
There was heat behind my eyes
My pupils expanded
Dark little mirrors widening in delight
A tear trickled down each cheek
Shining ruby-red against my pale skin
A warm hand trailed commanding fingers up and down my spine
Playing each knobbly protuberance with expertise
Flesh and bone
Skin and sinew
Muscle and marrow
This is the only instrument worth playing

I drank again
My thirst was slaked
But now I drank not to satisfy an animal need
But for the simple pleasure of tasting such deliciousness

I wetted my lips
And then licked them clean with my careful tongue
Which missed no drop

Then I drank again
Gulping and gulping
Gulping down handful after handful
Of that sweet, fiery nectar

And the heat bloomed again
Exploding in my belly
A hot flower bursting open within me
Sending shivers through me
And again those expert hands played my body
Warm fingers twisting in my hair
Hot hands caressing my shoulders
Scorching lips moving from breast to belly to thigh

I drank again
And again
And again

Yvonne Carsley

The Two Elephants

One was called Jumbo and the other one called Sacha.
They both lived in the circus and were billed with Molly.
Jumbo and Sacha had a trainer who used to teach them tricks.
One day Sacha just sat down in the show,
Jumbo said to Sacha, 'Why don't you want to do your tricks?'
Sacha said to Jumbo, 'I'm tired of doing the tricks.
The trainer said to Sacha, 'If you don't do your tricks
I will send you back to the jungle in Africa.'
Sacha said to the trainer, 'I don't care,'
And the next day they were put on a boat
To take them back to the jungle in Africa.
Jumbo and Sacha were happy in the jungle
And they both lived to be a good age.

Lucy Jones

The Earhole Brigade

Am I going insane, or becoming abnormal -
Seeing masses of people who appear quite formal -
Except for a slight deformity
That no one can surely fail to see.
One arm is in a triangle position,
Stuck to the ear, as though on a mission
Of destruction of social niceties,
Conversing at length about trivialities.
Wherever I go, to escape is in vain,
On the streets, the buses, also the train,
Boarding transport the lunacy continues -
No rest for the wicked, it gives me the blues.
These wee machines are taking life over,
Like aliens destroying fields of clover,
Like one-armed bandits, people are addicted,
Making bad drivers who should be convicted.
Why I avoid owing one is perfectly clear,
I *don't* want a machine stuck to my ear,
I *don't* want to join the Massive Parade,
I *don't* want to join the 'Earhole Brigade'.

Kathleen Beckley

Atom

Majestically simple in its very form,
But smaller by far than any eye can see.
Purveyor of life in its mystic ways,
In truth how more perfect could an atom be?

Roger Flavell

A Fool's Lament

I come to a table . . . so beautiful laid
With silver dishes and crystal shades.
With white damask cloth and napkins too,
And food of love . . . to take my fill.

My host, with a wave, says take your place,
I sit with a smile upon my face.
As I sit, I look . . . upon the fare
And eagerly wait . . . to take my share!

I fill my plate with this food of love
Not listening to the warnings . . . from wisdom above.
Scoffing it down in wanton haste,
Can't get enough to fill my face.
Sending it down to fill the hole within . . .
Not realising that it's a sin!

Don't step on the ground where Satan hides,
Deceiver that he is, that feeds you lies.
He'll break your heart and then he'll run.
This is the way . . . he has his fun!
He'll watch your tears fall from your eyes,
Then he'll find another . . . who'll believe his lies.

Learn from this fool, who seeks to be loved
Keep your focus on God above.
He is the Truth, the Light and the Way . . .
And He will never, ever . . . lead you astray!

Sheila Darby

The Shepherds

Dark, cold,
Sheep in fold,
Rough, tough,
They'd had enough,
Those shepherds on the hill.

Long days,
Sheep grazed,
Little money,
Life's not funny
For shepherds on the hill.

Exhausted, worn,
Clothing torn
They'd saved the sheep
But could not sleep
Those shepherds on the hill.

Oh what a lot to have in life,
No prospects - only toil and strife,
And endless days and nights to pass,
And sheep to rescue, flocks to grass.

Then flashing lights - and trumpets sound
And they're transformed to holy ground.
Those shepherds from a humble start
Preferred by God, who knew their heart,

Dark, cold,
Sheep in fold,
World is dreaming,
Starlight beaming,
Streaming on the hill.

Shepherds dazed,
Stunned - amazed,
Full of fear,
The first to hear,
God's son
Has come
To Earth
And now is near.

Diana Coutts

Out Of This World

'To reach out and touch the face of God'

There was something different on
My screen, a blue globe
Was suspended.
It seemed that someone in
Outer space had looked at the
Globe which is Earth.

The amazing pictures showed details of
Mountains, sea and rivers.
Half the globe was dark
Shaded by the moon,
Whilst the other half
Glowed in brilliant sunshine.

Yet Earth is only one in the
Galaxy shared by Mars, Jupiter,
Pluto, Venus and others.
Is there life on them?
I wondered, overcome by the
Majesty I could see.

Men have gone fearlessly to
Land on the moon.
Someday fearless travellers
Would venture and risk their
Lives to find other forms
Of life on other planets.

How amazing that all this
Was created by God in
Six days.
Even more amazing is
The way we treat our precious
Inheritance,
Until destruction.

Hilary Moore

Calendar Of Celebrations

We've always cause for a celebration,
In every town across the nation.
We use the word party and set a date,
Any chance we get to celebrate.
A wedding day when many shed a tear,
An anniversary for every extra year.
There's one kids remember without fail -
Easter time with its Easter egg trail.
Trick or treat and dressing up on Hallowe'en,
Music and dancing with the carnival queen.
For those who graduate and the school-leavers,
The exam passers and the high achievers.
It boosts morale and makes us feel good,
Just like a proper get-together should.
Births of babies bring lots of *coo-chi-coo.*
It's the start of something different and new.
Every year we're older is marked with a birthday,
Sometimes cards and cakes are the only way.
Except when it's a special coming of age,
When we're given presents that cost a wage.
A sibling's house warming, they've fled the nest,
When you've finally passed your driving test.
Or if your works' dragon has just been fired!
At the end of our stint - when we've retired.
With all the festivities at Christmas time,
There's be plenty of food and mulled wine.
Another year is welcomed by New Year's Day and Eve,
This can depend on your faith or what you believe.
There's a box of chocolates and even a song,
With the name 'Celebration' they won't go far wrong.

Trav (Sharon Caradice)

Thomas

A special time we had today
our grandson, *Thomas*, came to stay
his smile to see is such a joy
to see him rush to get a toy
the biscuit tin to him is a must
we love him so and have his trust
he is nearly five, he has grown so fast
but our love for him will always last
his nursery school days are at an end
his first proper school is round the bend
I'm sure he will find it a friendly place
and he will keep his smiling face.

Michael Saban

Changes

Life was good when I was a lad
And there was just me and Dad
Changes came as time went by
Things were not the same

With feelings all mixed up inside
Not able to explain
No one could see that all I wanted
Was time and things we shared
Me and Dad.

M Simpson

Calling

(Croyland Abbey)

It was the winter wind,
blasting all with iced turbulence
in this off-season, timedrift place, this
abandoned dyke-link to the Welland
reedy-wrought for picnic view
in summer; now only Christmas-festive
is this stately village, once a town
where life seems only Monday-to-Saturday
Sunday at least still has the Abbey church:
hymned carolly, and fulsomely
to the Saviour's night of birth, beyond
only the far-from-festive
wind on the fen, calling.

Why was grand glory here
so long ago?
It was St Guthlac, *he* wanted here;
for him, the church to make men think, and dream
save, conserve the land; therein preserve their souls
stone-mortar them to the monastic pile
sanctioned by kings in perpetuity
for the communal good.

One monarch failed; here as everywhere
his soul is damned . . .
we see, still, a gaunt, as inchoate,
crow-clad, roofless nave
so many once-bright holy sites
lost and gone across the fen and wold
our secularising world
the mighty west front, figured grandly
boasts its splendour now to tourist cars far off
racing the birds along the dyke-high tarmac way
no mitred grandeur now, but somehow
our power of contemplation?
We are yet consoled

how *can* that be?

Chris Brookes

Alfonso's Afraid Of The Night

Alfonso can't read! Alfonso can't write!
Alfonso's afraid of the night!
Alfonso's afraid of he's not sure what,
I know why he does not!
Alfonso's afraid of being alone!
Alfonso's afraid to be on his own!
Alfonso's afraid of life! His life!
Alfonso's afraid of his life!

Alfonso will shout! Alfonso will swear!
Wave his arm high! Yell at the air!
But Alfonso's afraid of the night - the night!
Alfonso's afraid of the night!

Wisby Brinn

Imagine

Have you ever stopped to think
What it's like to really need a drink
And you can't move yourself near the bloody sink?
What it's like to lie in bed on a lovely day
And wait till someone decides to say,
'It's time you were up on this fine day.'
What it's like to desperately need the loo
And people are ignoring you
Then have the gall to call you a pain
Just cos you need to go again.
And when you've imagined all these and more
This one will really knock you to the floor.
To be hoisted like a sack of coal
Really would destroy your soul.
These things are faced by many with total aplomb
Maybe it's cos their self-belief has gone
Because they've been told so many times
'Please don't worry - you'll be fine.'

Pam Jolly

21 Today

Forward Press, the people's publisher, has come of age today
21 on the 21st September 2009, many congrats will come your way
A million poets have found success and many thanks will send
Publishing for the people by the people, may it never end.

Forward Press, pressed forward, challenging poets to be inspired,
Offering wonderful opportunities for printed poems to be admired.
With busy minds, busy pens and busy emails, submissions flew,
But oh what exhilaration when a book 'acceptance' came through.

In 1992 'The Awakening' was my first accepted poem success,
Listed in the book 'The Spirit Writes' has led to joy and happiness.
130 published poems are now listed in my name,
Enjoyed weekly when I read them out in church. Yes, that's fame!

Since retiring I enjoyed learning various forms of poetry new
In mags Poetry Now, Rhyme Arrival, Triumph Herald, Christian poetry too,
I am now completely dedicated, poetry is with me every day,
Feel honoured copies of your published books in six famous libraries stay.

Forward Press, you have found success, new poetry has found you,
Now the largest people's publisher in the world, it's amazing and it's true.
So how many corks will be popping, celebrating you're 21 with champagne,
Winners of your chosen 'favourite fifty poets' thanks to you,
Three cheers for Forward Press, for now having made our name!

Stella Bush-Payne

Candlelight Canvases

Candlelight canvases splashing refraction
Into the open eye's pupil'd contraction
Illuminates sprightly a rainbow's attraction
Yet one misplaced stroke goes without distraction.

Cook's recipe spoiled by ratio's weight rate
Upon the soft-tongued quick, tentative equate
Is cause for not much more than taste bud to abate
By piquant degree to duly ma . . . sti . . . cate.

Cool sculpture carved coarsely or warmly and smoothly
As hard-angled edges arrive near-abruptly
Under the slow thumb or flute-fingered fleetly
Slipping the scourged-scour to mind-pleat them neatly.

Overtured undertones piercing and thrumming
Intoxications or rhythmic mind-numbing
Fanfares from brassy-knecks as from heart's drumming
Then missing-a-beat or pitch . . . unspoiling what's coming.

But now turn to syntax in word-palette's contrast,
And blend it with seasons of spiced or bland repast;
Sing it out forte, piano, then broadcast
Just one word or syllable wrong . . . and it's lost!

James Parry

Greek Islands

Fragrant scents
That never leave you
Luscious pines
Beckoning your return
Capturing spirits of adventure
Night after night
Idyllic sunsets
Tempt the perfect morning breeze
To chill in splendour
Occasional thunder
Can't escape the beauty
That intoxicates the mind
In submissive serenity

Oh radiant country
Islands of the gods
Stories told as truths
How you excite me
Returning to your shimmering shores
Is so sweet
Life a mere
Heartbeat of wonder
Vibrant beaches
Washed down
With menus of desire
Hour after hour cavorting
In summer seas and summer nights
Till the echo
Of one's home land
Goose pimples through
New found jewellery
And sadly, gradually
Brings my glowing family home
To once again
Dream and then touch
The shimmering shores of Greece

Grant Bayliss

So Special

(Dedicated to Jennie and Mike Harman)

Always there to talk to
Always there when I need to cry
Always there to comfort me
When I have craved to say goodbye

Goodbye to all the tragedy
That I see upon this Earth
To release my heart from pressure
Letting go . . . means giving birth

The pain of dedication
In searching for my truth
I have the incredible answers
As I bequest my living proof

Proof of a brand new beginning
That lies deep within my soul
You are both a part of me
A segment that has made me whole

Thank you both so very much
For being kind in every way
You have given me the human touch
So that I . . . will never decay

The prize is such an innocent love
Nesting inside my inner self
There was a time when I just liked
To sit quietly on the shelf

There really is no stopping me now
I know I can truly fly
A soaring bird with mighty wings
Conquering the midnight sky

I cherish this amazing beauty
It shines so bright from within
My seeing equals believing
And knowing today I can win

Katrina Graham

View Some Days

High days, low days, away days, at home days,
Each and every one different in their own way.
On stirring from night's slumbers,
You just snuggle back down in bed
If your day is not specifically planned,
You ponder what might be in store ahead.
Breakfast, chores, first come to mind,
Shopping, meals to plan,
Maybe a school run to arrange,
A fête, to help where'er you can.
You look up to the heavens,
Wishing to see a sky of blue,
Spirits lifted, the sun beheld,
Now so many things to do.
Some days you feel downhearted,
Your world appears so drear and not so bright,
When everything you attempt to do seems so onerous,
At the end then not right.
You endeavour to lift your spirits up,
Play music, strive to do an absorbing task.
You flounder further into the doldrums,
Perchance, in grief you bask.
Take a moment of reflection, count your blessings,
Be astonished at what you find.
Just be grateful for so many things,
Your family, your friends, kindnesses recalled to mind.
Make a comforting warm drink,
Be it coffee, chocolate or tea,
Your mood uplifted, your thoughts refined,
Look about and see
Nature's display of flowers and trees,
Birds on the wing, cloud sailing on high,
Your low day now progressive give a smile, a happy sigh
Look forward to an away day, visit friends or family,
Perchance a sunny day at the seaside, or even new clothes to buy.
Maybe an especial holiday, a wedding,
Christening or anniversary,
Each day is our life's blessing,
Our delight, you must agree.

Marjorie Leyshon

Twenty-One Today

Twenty-one, the key of the door,
You've opened many a door before.
Forward Press have led the way
For unknown poets to have their say.

Be it prose or in rhyme,
You have given us your time.
Printing in a special book
For all to buy and take a look.

May you continue to seek us out,
Finding talent - that's what it's about.
Thank you editors and all concerned,
Your faith in us we have truly earned.

So now enjoy your celebrations,
Keep us in print - *congratulations!*

Enid F Thomas

No One Told Me

Breakfast is ready and you are late
rush to school now my child
where you will learn your fate
but first give me a hug and kiss before time runs wild
no one told me this would be our last
you were smiling and happy last time I saw your face
never thinking our time together would soon be past
and you would be playing in a heavenly place
when through the howling wind and driving rain
I heard the sirens wail
And my heart felt a searing pain
As I watched people running to no avail
To our village of Aberfan where a school once stood
And where our children now in silence lay
Pausing a moment to whisper goodbye
Before going to play in Heaven's night skies
Where they will forever be
Our stars.

Jan Maissen

The Long Walk

I have sisters, yes I do
I love them dearly, you and you
But oh what a scream, a hullabaloo
When we get together, me, you and you.

Then there's my sister's dog, Lucy by name
It's terrible, a crying shame.
She thinks she's large, and full of flame
But she is a little terrier; Lucy by name
I flew up to Scotland to see these three;
My sister's dog Lucy, you, you and me
We went for a walk down by the sea
When all I wanted was a cup of tea.
I was made to sit on a stone and gaze
At birds and shells all in a haze
My throat was dry, in a thirsty phase
I wanted a cuppa but was told to gaze.

I then continued to walk the beat,
With Lucy, you and you, in the heat
When other dogs passed by at our feet
Lucy the Lion saw them retreat.

At last, Heaven appeared before me
The sight of home and a cuppa tea
Lucy was worn out; don't you see
But bliss, oh bliss, I had my cup of tea!

Vanessa Laws

Heaven

What is Heaven? Up above?
Something in the sky?
We humans here upon the Earth,
We live a while, then die.

Where do we go? Our bodies gone -
They're burned or buried here.
The brains we have just cease to exist.
They stop, with pain and fear.

The suffering we feel down here
Is usually just Hell.
The brain controls the state we're in
If we become unwell.

Is Heaven just a hazy dream
Where we can waft in bliss?
Or do we need a human hand?
Or even just a kiss?

I do not know what to expect,
Or what I'll ever find.
Can anybody tell me,
To get it off my mind?

Doris E Pullen

Angel Voice

Radiant
And beautiful
She sat there
Looking down
Letting go
The gold dust
From the
Purest high
Twisting and
Twirling
She flew
Across the trees
She came across
A lonely man
Who didn't want
To speak
She sat down
Beside him
And looked
Into his eyes
The sadness
She could see
Lurking behind
'Please, let me
Help you,'
Came the
Angel voice.
The man stood up
And slowly
Walked away.
That night
The angel
Stood by
His bed,
'I shall
Help you
While you sleep,'
She softly
Said.
The next day

Arrived
And the man
Went to
The shop
'Lucky dip
For tonight
And also
Please
Put these
Numbers on.'
When he won
His millions
He couldn't
Understand
Why.
He always dreamt
Of an angel
Close by
Now
She was gone
He wondered why.
The angel
Smiled.
Her work was done
She was
Ready
To let
The gold dust
Choose
The next one!

Sharon Lambley

Elegy For A Slain Forest

A forest marched across the land,
From riverside to coast it spread,
Its blend of modest trees - and grand,
Each spring, through swathes of fresh flow'rs tread;
(Here countless wildlife played and bred.)

A coppice clothed a rugged hill,
Where now a road was threaded through,
But handsome trees bore witness still
To that great forest which once grew;
(Some wildlife now, is absent too.)

A solitary beech looked down
From hillside field where cattle grazed,
A village growing to a town,
Was now the view on which it gazed:
(More wildlife still, has been erased.)

Great towns and cities cross the land,
From motorways to coasts they've grown,
Lone trees that have been left to stand,
Mark pages of an era known;
(Wildlife is in extinction zone.)

Lorena Triggs

Future Thoughts

As before with my arms hugging
And hands clasping
I hold my unread biography
Tightly to protect it,
Lest the wind of change
Shall catch the pages
And scatter them;
Scattering also my thoughts
About an unforeseen future
Which I would try to remain wishful
Would be of my life
As I would want it to be.

Kevan Beach

Seaside Cottage Garden

Cottage garden, an artist's pleasure,
Sunshine, tranquillity, gently blows sea breeze,
Perfume pervades an utter treasure,
Insects mystical, eyeing enactment frieze.

Pollen-hunting, abseiling brimmed bees,
Bewitching butterflies dancing a ballet,
Some birds swooping up and down with glee,
Preparing to fly to warmer clime sunrays.

Mountaineering spiders weaving lace,
Ensnaring naïve prey in filigree web,
Dewdrops glowing bright as a showcase,
Lighting drop lanterns as halcyon days ebb.

Awesome in midst of painter's palette,
Wondrous to see and learn, rustling up quiet time,
Sights viewed and sounds of nature's secrets,
Droll entertainment by well-cast pantomime.

Hilary Jill Robson

My Sisters

God gave to me three sisters.
A blessing, that is true.
We did not always see eye to eye;
but then, sisters never do.
We would consult, confide and copy.
We would compete, encourage or blame.
We would conspire, bicker or be nasty
and learned there was no shame
in expressing disapproval of childish subterfuge,
or telling one another
if we found something was 'really good'.

We never fought like cat and dog
or pulled each other's hair
but we loudly protested and told the world
when something was not fair.
We never scratched each other's eyes out
or stepped on one another's toes.
If we could not agree or compromise,
then our mum heard all our woes.

She, herself had had five sisters
and loved each and every one,
and in her worldly wisdom
knew that sisters could be fun.
The childish, petty squabbles can be nasty, hurtful too,
But a sister's love is a blessing,
and can last your whole life through.
Providing you remember that you're her sister too.

Of course the teenage years were a minefield
for each and every one.
We suddenly became emotionally charged
with no thought for anyone.
As we discovered boys and fashion,
make-up and the rest,
we thought that we had learned it all
as we prepared to fly the nest.

We would express outrageous notions
that shook the family to the core;
then throw an almighty tantrum
when we should have been shown the door.

But no, there was always one sister
who would take us quietly aside
to talk the whole thing over and perhaps we would decide
That the only one that we had hurt,
was ourselves with our foolish pride.

The years rolled on; now they have gone, my sisters, everyone.
All the drama and the tantrums when all is said and done.
I miss my lovely sisters. All their laughter and their fun.

Bridget Taber Beeson

High And Low

St Vitus
Dancing on high
Mucha blue in a too bright, piercing, gashing, glass sky
Telephone, telephone, telephone chatter
Words and words, thumping, clatter
Nicotine rush
Adrenalin glow
Caffeine whoosh
Alcohol flow
Go with the glow
Go with the glow
Go, go, go with the glow
Sedative shush
Sedatives whisper
Sedative shush
Sedative hush
Sedatives shush
Sedatives shush
Sedatives whisper
Whisper, whisper,

Whimper.

Caroline Kemp

The Story Of Eve

It belonged to a soft-bodied creature of
peachy pink.
It sat beneath sand and mud and clay.
I did not learn this until I grew.

At first I just imagined.
I imagined it came from a
shell tree -
where tiny creatures wore
gems of emerald and ruby.
They danced inside spirals of bubbles.
I'd hear the flow of splashes
echo back.
I'd want to scream, 'Hello!'
as I placed it onto the tablecloth.

I named it Eve.
Over time it began to scare me.
My uncle had given it to me -
I had forgotten to give it back.
He had died.
What if he came back through Eve?

I'd listen,
I held the smooth, spotted base against my ear lobe.
The spikes and jagged branches
edged through my hair.
I ached to listen.
I'd dream he'd shrunk and gone to sit with Eve.
To speak to other spirits, or think.
There was a forest of pines covered
in snow.
When you drew breath it was pure cold -
ice frosted your eyelashes.
I pulled the duvet closer.
The next day I hid Eve.
I grew older.

I found Eve beneath a matted, muddied flip-flop,
sand glued to the shell.
I remembered.
So I placed her into the sand
with the mud and the clay.

Now she can be kissed by the neons'
and guppies' feathery tails,
and I can hear the echoes of the sea.

Rose Edmondson

Naked Trees

Smoke from bonfires burning,
crackling leaves;
autumn breeze
blows.
Playing tricks with debris
lying in piles at the foot of naked trees.
Autumn games are mischievous,
her moody interludes devious.
Obeying without reason
coping with a change of season;
time for leaves and flowers to die.
The breeze has changed its course,
and force.

Now battle rages,
as nature wages
war against the silent trees.
Oak, beech and ash,
skeletal sentries
bending, bowing
against the strength of an unseen enemy.
Brittle branches fall, snapping in the wind.
Broken, fractured joints caught in currents,
drowning in advancing air.
Dropping to the ground,
creaking groans, echoed moans
of injured wooden bones,
soon to fuel the fire
when placed upon the pungent pyre.
Ashes to ashes.

Ann Wardlaw

On Long-Remembered Love

Freckled sun through half-closed lashes,
time taken captive as the years unravel -
half in sorrow for past years lost and half in joy
the sweet rose-tint of memory paints long gone days
                              in pastel shades -
an artist's hand, your cherished hand, upon the canvas of my life.

The unseen birds that stilled our hearts and limbs
for fear our breath might interrupt the show
seem now through mists of time to sing, with voices
                              warmed by golden sun,
and kissing-gates for years unmoved swing creaking
                              on a rusty hinge -
and your dear face, your dear, kind face, recalls in me
                              the brief embrace.

No bridge for dry-brogued weekend hikers -
a river crossed on stepping stones and trembling feet,
and slipping shoes, muddied reeds and safety -
laughing, grateful for the rest, fern deep and wood musk,
                              water's edge -
and you my love, and you my love, in sun-washed,
                              silver-dappled light.

Sun-ripened skin and your sunburned hands;
I'd hover as a held breath . . . and shiver in the summer haze -
then take flight with other busy wings, swept high
as though the moment was a dream, with clouds
                              and branches overhead -
in poppy fields, red poppy fields did all my summers come.

Long sun-stretched shadows running on,
we'd try to catch and still our precious time
but though we ran we stayed one step behind;
the same long shadows now as then escape elusive as the wind -
but you my love, my precious love, cast no dark shadows
                              in my dreams.

When age and time no longer count the years between
sweet memories and long gone care-worn days,
then endlessly will rivers run again and kissing gates
                              swing free in poppy fields.

But now I wait - and as my summer sun descends
I'll live my days, my autumn days, among the leaves
of let's pretend.

Linda Kernot

It's Not Murder On The Dance Floor

Strictly every Thursday at 7 o'clock
I don my shoes but not the frock
To do the Samba and Cha Cha Cha
On the floor I feel a star
But mastering the Foxtrot and the Waltz
I really feel so very false
My technique's not right
And it may take all night
But I'm eager to learn
To know which way to turn
Doing the Tango I creak my neck
But what the heck
Though it's not the Argentine
With legs entwined
We go back to the forties and do the Jive
It's so energetic but I feel really alive
I've even been taught by the Strictly pros
They never once stood on my toes
If those judges were here
I'd be dancing in fear
Would I get a ten
From Alesha, Craig, Bruno and Len?
Dancing in the old-fashioned way
Was the highlight of my parents' day
Now Ballroom and Latin are back in fashion
And I just love my dancing with a passion.

Janet Bedford

Abingdon's Alder

Great moaning in the treetops set a-sway
brought wizened alder branches crashing down -
felled, unattended, here in Abingdon town,
all in the wailing winds of yesterday.
And as they plunged my thoughts flew instantly
to Nature's Clare, his murmuring elm they axed -
untimely death to suit a government act,
all in the wailing winds of yesterday.
So *Abyngdone* gave up to powers its abbey and might -
as Plowman foretold - then lost its waterway,
lido, rail link, film house, fields and rights,
all in the wailing winds of yesterday.
But Helen's prophets emerged, and great foresight
lets the red kite soar on our winds today.

Susan Biggin

A View So Fine

I have climbed the Monros, roamed the Glens,
explored the Lakes, the Dales and Fens.
I have toured the Broads and Wolds and Wealds,
and Stately Homes and Battlefields.
I have sauntered over Downs and Moors,
and tramped the paths which hug our shores.
But there's one very special place where my footsteps slow
and my heartbeats race.
For ahead of me lies a view so fine, I savour it like vintage wine.
I drink and drink, can't get my fill, of the wondrous sight that's Dedham Mill.

Neil Pollard

Thwarted Ambition

I'm a marrow and I'm stuffed
And not feeling very chuffed
For it ain't funny
Being served up on a plate.
I lie steaming hot and raging
Agonised and waiting
For that steely slicing moment
Which will decide my fate.
My savoury rice filling
Doesn't find it very thrilling,
Nor the cheese tomato topping,
Which has really run amok.
I'm so livid, mad and seething
And I've got this funny feeling
I'm in this sad predicament
Cos I just ran out of luck.
I'm shocked and broken-hearted,
My consume-ation will be soon,
Please spare a thought
For a sad little marrow
Who's filled with rice and doom and gloom.
I can't believe that gardener picked me,
For I hadn't even reached full size.
And if I'd only been given
The chance to grow
I'd have been *the Best*
And *Biggest marrow*
In the County Show
And *I know* I would have won
First Prize!

Margaret Lygo-Hackett

Night-Time In Oberndorf

The night closed in on Oberndorf,
Made stencil shapes of mountain peaks
That added to the skyline frieze.
An Austrian valley soon to have
Its meadows in the twilight zone.
The unknown future flowed towards
This present moment held in time.

A nightly entertainment booked;
Male actors lederhosen clad,
Performed with energy, folk songs,
Combined with dances: superb acts.

We left the hall and headed back
Across the meadows, hand in hand,
Upon a land, not of this world,
Or, so it seemed, as midnight cast
Its awesome spell; accompanied
By moonlight softer than a sigh
That follows on from utter bliss.
We lingered on the wooden bridge
Which spanned the rapid running stream;
Its blackened surface glistening
With dancing images of stars.

The hotel loomed before our eyes
To welcome us with sleep and dreams.
We looked back at the scene we'd left:
Those timbered houses, cafés, shops,
With ancient church proclaiming peace,
And glowing from the full moon's rays.

The influence of Oberndorf,
More permanent than memory.

Raymond W Seaton

Our Colourful Masks

Masks we wear hide a thousand tears
As colours depict our mood for the day
And sat alone we work our way through our fears
Still clinging to the hope in the words others say

Knowing we could have been a contender
For all the things great we dreamed of for years
Dreaming of the loves we lost, so warm and tender
Haunted by the ghosts that were not so fair

Sometimes the trivial things seem larger than they are
But nothing is truly minute if you look carefully
Wanting the moon when you have every star
So golden and soft, each crafted beautifully

Several days go by intertwining with each other
Seconds drag; sometimes like years
But they can never erase the memories of you as my lover
Now I'm left wondering if you really cared.

I see the brownness of your eyes each time I close mine
I even smell your aroma each time I enter a room
And I have to bite my lip each time I smile
Wishing we didn't have to end so soon

So many questions run through my head
About where I must go from here
Searching endlessly for every word you said
Finding solace at the bottom of my bottle of beer

But I know that's not the route to take
Therefore in memory of you I shall resist
But still those emotions I wish you did not fake
For even with my love for you; you will always be missed

So now sweet angel; my love, to you I say
I hope you can smile for the rest of all time
For if you're right I shall move forward one day
Knowing just briefly, a part of you was mine.

Graham Connor

My Dad

Dad is so special to me, I'm sure you'll agree
When I was a child
We travelled afar, my dad, my mother, brother and me,
To Cornwall,
Wales,
Scotland too
From Derbyshire to Land's End
And to Chester Zoo
We had to stop for every loo
We went up Flamborough lighthouse
And I screamed and screamed
And held everyone up
My dad held out his arms and was there for me
When I was a teenager there were times I let him down
My dad was hurt, but with a smile and a frown
He didn't let me down
When I was a child I was full of life
We danced, sang and did acrobatics
Dad did them too, he did a handstand up the outhouse door
He couldn't get down
We weren't sure where he would land
So we had to give him a hand
My dad, he's so generous and kind
I started writing this before he died.
He had a good sense of humour and was quick-witted too
He could fix most anything
And became a great grandad
He was loved so much and still is
And he will always be my dad.

Christine Angela Austin

Credit Crunch

Gradually gaining physical energy,
As gas and electricity fuel bills rise,
Incapacity benefit, abrupt stop,
As credit crunches autumn leaves under feet.

Supportive crutch lost, feel cheated, angry, crushed,
Does cup size fit all, need alteration, trust?
On cusp of change, challenge, opportunity,
Chance for more hours, builds wealth of stamina.

Vibrant leaf shades in park, if God clothes nature
Will cover my aching chest for other's needs,
In perspective, accepting limitations,
Knowing God's security, can stand alone.

Helen Howard

Soft Focus

Carefree lovers in the square
Spin artless magic in the air.
They live in dream worlds all their own,
Worlds we can no longer share.

Their lives quicksilver escapades
To flirt, disport and date,
To hold each other's hands, bemused in awe,
And mouth sweet nothings no one else may hear.

Their smouldering love takes fire with a kiss,
Inflames them into feverish embrace,
Coiled in each other's arms they melt in bliss
Unconscious of whatever else exists.

We cannot gauge their shallows or their deeps,
The torrents of their wild exuberance,
We are forever out of reach
Dismayed by love's untamed concupiscence.

Ray Racy

Twenty-One Now

This garden of flowers so pretty and bright,
Bonding together and bringing in light
Pretty zinnias and roses and daffodils too
Which amaze the people as they walk through.

These flowers which you sow and propagate
Give such pleasure and we must not underrate,
Our hearts are filled just pottering around,
And as for this exercise it's vitally sound.

When in our heart of hearts we try
'Forward Press' you are flying high,
Started slowly but surely you have arrived
Worked very hard and God is on your side.

May the God of sunshine visit you now,
And may His grace shine on your brow
Twenty-one now but only just,
You are thriving ahead, so what is the fuss?

Give thanks at dawn and at the dusk,
For light, food and flowers and you must,
With courage and care, share some blessings too,
It is with goodness that He gives to you.

M S Joseph

The Happy Hookers

About a quarter of a century ago
A group of friends decided they would start
A crochet group - to meet just once a month
And learn how best to use this ancient art.

Though we have lost some members on the way
We're still meeting and the group is going strong
With wool and crochet hooks or knitting needles
We sit and knit and natter all night long.

Our hostess gives us 'lubberly grub' to eat
And with a cup of coffee or of tea
We happily enjoy our monthly treat.

We save some cash each month and twice a year
We hire a minibus and off we go
To have an evening meal with wine somewhere,
Just something to look forward to, you know.

Our December meeting turns into a party
With food that we have all made in our cookers,
And as we say, 'Good night and happy Christmas,'
We're all a lot of very *happy hookers!*

Peggy Seeley

Twenty-One Years Of Publishing Poetry

There are 21 very good reasons
why I am writing this today
The wonderful people at Forward Press
wrote me a letter to say

They have been publishing poetry
for people just like me
who enjoy the art of writing
for all the readers to see

Just what individuals thought about
the iambic pentameters too
I really like my poetry
to 'bounce' along - don't you?

My favourite kind of poetry
for there are so many kinds
are the ones that rhyme at the ends of lines
or any other style - I just don't mind

I love to write my poems
when I'm happy or when I'm sad
the emotions just flow out through my pen
it really makes me glad

To share my thoughts with others
who like to have a read
and think, *well that's a nice poem*
all I needed was the seed

Or ending for a line or two
then I just fill in the blanks
so let me wish you all the best
and just pass on my thanks

Michelle Broadbent

Wing-ed Gems

Flutter by
Butterfly
Flutter by

Do your dance
In the sky
Butterfly

Sometimes here
Sometimes there
Wing-ed gems
In the air

Flutter by
Butterfly
Flutter by

Flutter by
Butterfly
Flutter by

As you flit here and there
In the sky
You bring so much delight
To the eye

Flutter by
Butterfly
Flutter by

Flutter by
Butterfly
Flutter by

But your beauty is brief
Like a glowing autumn leaf

Flutter by
Butterfly
Flutter by.

R J McCulloch

The Pathway Of Life

This pathway of life doesn't always run smoothly.
Setbacks, disappointments and disagreements can litter the way.
But we try to keep going, there's no turning back.
Life is not always glum, we can be blessed with happier days.

Life is a gamble, we take what it throws at us, though sometimes,
At the crossroads, we can make our own decisions
To make the best use of our journey here
And hope that good fortune is with us, at least part of the way.

But for all of its ups and downs I wouldn't have missed
The chance to be a part of this world, this wonderful world
With all that is in it. Not all of it good, not all of it bad.
Sometimes we are happy, sometimes sad, but we have to take what fate
hands out.

To see the sun rise in the early morn is a spectacle not to be missed,
It appears like a huge red ball, slowly turning into gold.
Suddenly the whole resembles an overflowing melting pot of running
molten gold.
Soon the brilliant light like a bowl of sparkling diamonds is too strong for the
naked eye.

The sky on a dark night is filled with twinkling stars,
Another of great Nature's wonderful sights.
The moon, ever the lovers' friend, but she sometimes hides
Behind the nearest cloud. We wonder what goes on up there?

I have known the Yorkshire moors on a sunny, windless day,
With the heather-laden hills in the distance, a beautiful picture to see.
I have known the moors in a much less happier mood,
When the wind, in a fury, has blasted the land like a savage suddenly let loose.

I have had the pleasure of flying high above the clouds to distant lands.
I have sailed the heaving oceans to faraway places,
All while travelling on this road of life.
I have seen huge mountain ranges standing rigid, like an army of warriors
'Don't disturb us.'

Mother Nature can be cruel as well as kind.
On the plains of Africa the wild beasts tear each other up for food,
That is Nature's way.
While in the river the giant-jawed crocs lay in wait for their prey,
While the mother croc gently tends her young.

To hear the music of the great composers such as Brahms, Beethoven and Bach, is
to hear Heaven's music itself.
To see the magnificent cathedrals, and the stately piles
Of the titled rich, gives one a glimpse of Britain's past history.

Yes, this is a varied, interesting and unique world.
The path may be long or short but we grasp it whilst we can.
Yes, Dylan, I shall not go gently into that goodnight,
Unless the pathway takes a different turn, then I might be glad to see the fading
of the light.

Ann Ashworth

The Fading Of The Green

I look from attic window and, surprised, I see
The leaves of green are changing on my greenest tree.
How wistfully they don their gay array
Of flaming rust and glaring gold -
How sadly now they bow and sway,
With desperation they are growing old.
Moist winds dance spitefully around my shaking tree
And all the leaves cry, 'Hush!' against profanity!
What whisperings I hear across the lane
Of summer loves and loves untold -
What echoes of an instant's pain
Fly never-ending in eternal cold.
For a loved one I sigh as I hark to my tree -
'Don't mourn so,' it cries, 'for a love which leaves thee.'
Becalmed once more, it rustles fingers dry;
A few leaves flutter to the ground -
My hopes and summer gently die;
I bow my heart, and wait for winter's sound.
I gaze from attic window, and I sadly see
The leaves of green have vanished from my greenest tree.

Thelma Welham

Peace Poem

My time's come
to signal end.
I'll not be here
tomorrow, friend.
Hwaet!
        I bequeath.
Your choice?
        To spend.

Fire and ice
we both need
to learn how best
to sow our seed
in wonder-tales.
It's why we breed.

Myths create us
right or wrong -
in hoards of words,
in lure of song
and art in caves.
So?
In love be strong.

Veronica Anne

Beast

His mouth, like a black orchid,
opens to her stars.

His claws, like cats' tongues,
surprise her petal skin.

His fur, like lichen on the rocks,
entices her hesitant hand.

His teeth, like an owl's wings,
trace the rhythm of her heart.

His eyes, like whale-song,
yearn for newborn young.

Liz Muir

May Day, Stotfold 2009

Before dawn, birds were singing
in the lamp-lit high street trees,
and a slender fox wandered by!
In Etonbury Wood I saw a badger,
and several young rabbits playing.
Just after 5.30, on the distant horizon,
the May Day sun emerged from low mist
into a clear blue sky.
As it rose higher and brighter,
silvery dewdrops and spiders' silk
shone all over the grass by my feet.
Cycling along I thought about Morris men
greeting the day with traditional dance,
leaping about in flower-bedecked hats!
Ickwell children would be rising early
to dance around the maypole on the green,
weaving and unweaving ribboned patterns
as they changed direction on damp grass,
before going home for breakfast, then school!
Cycling a short way along the A507,
with little traffic at this early hour,
I stopped to photograph wild cowslips,
which this year have been especially good.
Leaving the road I cycled along grassy tracks
to the Pix Brook nature reserve.
Here the large golden king cup flowers
grow in several spots around the lake,
which is bordered by tall bullrushes,
their woody stems and fluffy seed heads
all reflected in the clear water
glistening blue under the cloudless sky.
I cycled home past the Fox and Duck,
opening under Ted Saunders' ownership today,
it's Devonshire cream coloured walls
enhanced with flower baskets and barrels.
It deserves a bright, successful future,
providing good food and entertainment,
a meeting place for us all to enjoy!

Patricia Anne Ray

Dumbing Down

What ancient, cruel, recessive gene
Has made me less than tall,
That takes my blood to boiling point
When's said that I am small?

The mirrors are above my head
I cannot check my teeth
Were I to suffer bloodshot eyes
I'm spared the disbelief.

The gas stove has eye-level grill
If you are six foot two
I stand upon a kitchen stool
So I can see it too.

The dining chairs are rather low
The table rather high
My knife and fork do vital work
But level with my eye.

I thought I ought to have a car
Or I would be left out
I sought one with a periscope
So I could see about.

I found a distant showroom
With cars and cars galore
The salesman, he was talkative
But less than five foot four.

I told him of my penchant
The problems held in store
He said, 'No trouble, darlin'
You need a four-by-four.'

Bill let me climb into the seat
Describing all the levers.
We took it for a gentle drive
But men are such deceivers . . .

He hugged me close to fit the belt,
The sat-nav in my eyes
And then he took a kiss or two
That was a big surprise.

I said I really liked the car
The vision was extensive
A papal wave I could bestow -
But was the brute expensive?

The four-by-four is now my own
Bill works a seven-day week
I drive about like Madam Muck
I'm too high up to speak.

Sarah Brown

August

It's August,
And already Summer
Shows his autumn face.
The moorhen's cry
Echoes across
The still-life pond,
And the dry leaves
Whisper and roar
On the muscled branches
Reaching to the sky.
The furtive sun
Slips silently behind
The wind-swept clouds,
Whilst swallows somersault
Overhead on their final
Journey of the year.

Josephine Thomas

Laughter

Laughter should bubble through the inn
Where true ale slakes the folk within
And friendly banter, cautioned wit
Proclaims the English part of it.

Laughter should strike the village bell
Fulsome with knowledge that all is well
And echo, echo until mankind
Is resonant, reborn, refined.

Laughter should float across the plain
And lighten labour, ease the strain,
Would touch the heart of hardened soul
So love renew its age-old goal.

Laughter should bounce around in space
Delicate as finest lace
Or make a lattice to the stars
Yet blind the weaponry of Mars.

Laughter should ripple like the waves
Lost in the depths of unplumbed caves,
Returned, to touch a million shores
And shroud the bones of former wars.

Laughter should break that final spell
Where hatred puts all souls through hell;
Venom, vendetta, puffing pride.
Let love and laughter push aside.

Laughter should tumble as mountain stream
Where birds flee crevices and scheme
To catch a fly upon the wing
Then perch and sing, and sing and sing.

Laughter should tremor a cabbage rose
Then sprinkle dew about your toes
Or rise upon a morning mist
To greet those heroes died unkissed.

Laughter should sparkle like magic dust
Thrown on the stage of life and thrust
Into the wind of change to shower
Mankind with God's ennobling power.

C Maskall Williams

124

Akrostikhis

P ardon me poet! What did you say? What
E xactly did your words convey?
R epeat in plain English so that I can understand,
F or modern poetry is refreshing but sometimes bland.
E veryone has a style to express their thoughts, but
C larity of meaning is what is sought.
T o deal with the long, make it short.
L ines with rhymes are easier to remember,
Y es, and gives the reader less time to ponder. The

P assing shadows of the night flee away
O n the dawn of a new and beautiful day. The
E clectic old man sits amongst his garden trees,
T hinking of the times he could paint what he sees.
I t's the eyes, the window to the world, that have deserted him,
but the eyes are also the mirror of the soul that look within,
So, with paintbrush in hand, and with swirling brushstrokes,
he makes his mark - the result
C ontentment, complete satisfaction and birdsong so
enchanting, refreshes the spirit and is deeply calming.

Eileen Beatrice Johnson

Angel

When your heart's getting broken some more,
And you don't think your life's worth living for,
And all the pain inside just won't fade away,
Can't seem to find the strength to live another day

I will be there for you
You know I'm there for you
I'll still be there for you
To help you see it through

And when you're down
And there's no one else around,
And when you're low,
Seems like there's no place to go,
I will be there for you.

Laurence Richards

A Lady

'Come to tea,' she said.
We ate and ate with ravenous content
Of these sandwiches, with crusts cut off,
And scrumptious fillings: cucumber,
Paste and real butter, and napkins white,
White as snow.
She talked and talks of days long gone,
Of wondrous things, and all the time
Her fingers were not still.
She had this little sewing bag,
Tidying cottons and things.
And in-between we ate home-made cakes
With butterfly wings.
The time flew by, we had to go.
'See you next week.'
I kissed her cheek.
The silver-haired lady with a lovely smile,
Was a true lady.

Claudette Evans

The Message

Preserving the world is the message today
Environment issues the task force will say
Recycle your waste and do your best
It is the only way to get out of this mess
We must think green and go with the scheme
Conserving energy is the Final dream
Nature could go bust unless we trust
In developing this situation
We'll save the nation.

Linda Elizabeth Morgan

Happiness

My heart is filled with happiness -
When I behold the first bright primrose in a grassy bank,
Or see some cowslips nodding bravely in the hedge,
And hear a blackbird singing to his mate
Upon a pleasant evening in the spring.

My heart is filled with happiness -
Whilst walking on a Cornish beach to see
The huge Atlantic breakers crashing on the shore
And hear the seabirds wheel and cry above
And feel the damp, warm sand between my toes.

My heart is filled with happiness -
When I can watch a buzzard hovering above the moor,
Or hear a river rushing to the sea,
Splashing and bubbling in the morning sun
And watch a dipper bobbing on a stone.

My heart is filled with happiness -
When singing in a choir, great requiems
Gerontius, Messiah - so many other works;
With orchestra or organ in cathedral, church or hall.
Excitement, elation, sadness and joy too.

My heart is filled with happiness -
To hold my darling cat and hear him purr.
Or watch our dogs playing upon the beach
To have my dearest children close to me
And feel their love and friendship through the years.

Ann Linney

Jennifer's All-Day Hen Party

Jennifer's all-day hen party was held at Boscundle Manor.
The invite said, *Come on girls, let's get pampered.*
On arrival we had the red carpet treatment.
Then ushered into the breakfast room for tea, coffee, cereal and croissants.
After breakfast fourteen girls gaily trooped upstairs to the pool room
Where bags and baggage were dropped in tumbled confusion.
Amidst fun and laughter, several girls went swimming,
Others sat around the pool, drinking coffee and relaxing.
Steam rose from the hot tub which was very popular.
I'm not sure if I was pushed or pulled in - an experience to remember.
Pampering sessions were being arranged by Kirstie and Zoë
When we were told lunch was ready in the conservatory.
Down three flights of stairs, to a beautifully laid table
Where plates of assorted sandwiches and salad were available.
Waiters filled glasses with pink champagne and Buck's Fizz
And to the girls' delight, followed by chocolate fondue dip.
Everyone chatting and happy, sitting around the table
Teasing Jenny with cheeky remarks which ended with us all in giggles.
After coffee, upstairs again for our pampering sessions of
Pedicures, facial make-up and body massage,
Painted finger and toenails in a colour of choice
By caring trained assistants, who were helpful with advice.
Soon it was time to shower, pack bags, then downstairs for tea.
At five o'clock, after a lovely day, it was time to leave.
Rushing home to get ready for the meal at the Pier House Hotel
With Jennifer's many friends, Mum, Pat and family as well.
Dressed with a sash, red feather boa, blue veil and tiara,
Jennifer laughed with her friends at the cheeky jokes and witty banter.
It was a wonderful evening, with good food and good friends,
And the longest hen party I have been asked to attend.

Lorna June Burdon

Neil

As dawn broke in the sky the young man strode on by,
Across the field and up the hill
Up past the trees stark and bare,
Up and onwards he knew not where,
His lean, hard body bent against the morning chill,
His grey eyes hard as steel.
He paused to ponder for a while,
What had fate in store for him?

Should he move to the town, his fortune to amass
Imprisoned in the world of greedy men,
With tiny houses row upon row and neat gardens all fenced in,
Cars and lorries nose to tail, smoke and fumes to inhale?
Or should he stop where he belongs,
Wild and free and strong?

In anguish the young man lifted his eyes up to the sky
And as if by magic the sun's rays lit up the trees so stark and bare
The birds began to sing.
He breathed in the fresh morning air of spring.
A smile appeared upon his lips, a sparkle in his eye.
The ground felt good beneath his feet,
His heart with happiness did beat.
He knew what fate had in store for him.

I mourned the passing of my days,
For I surely would have beside him stayed.
The earth to feed with sweat and blood, and water with our tears.
As the seasons rolled way and our hair turned silver-grey
I would have lived my life no other way.

Rose M Clay

England, Our England

Land of hope and glory,
England is unique.
There is so much lovely countryside
if you care to peek.

The changing seasons,
have a beauty all their own;
like an interwoven tapestry,
that has been lovingly sewn.

There are hidden treasures
down a leafy lane,
wild flowers in the hedgerows -
just look again and again.

Sprawling farmland and rivers,
picturesque cottages and the seaside.
Large cities and small towns,
the diversity is wide.

Close-knit communities,
the friendly church meeting.
Wherever you wander,
our England has a greeting.

Gloria S Beeston

This Raging Raven

This raging raven will not fly,
no good men can face it, only I.

Though good men I know will
always wish,
they could throw the bird into
distant flight.
For they have seen me cry through
night-time plight,
screaming and begging, 'Die raven, die.'

Yes, the blackest of birds is
always there
to pass his judgement on what he
thinks fair.
Not to sing or soar on high,
but to punish me and bring despair.

What crueler passing can there be,
than to spur me on and watch me fall?
And for the good men to cry as they
hear me call,
leave me alone, and die raven, die.

Matthew O'Dwyer

Windows

This wall seems too high to climb
Sleeping this dream when is the time
I'll get to the top
How did this start?
Why should this stop?
Waiting to be up looking around
To feel no distance between
Myself and the ground
I could work with nature's gravity
She who keeps down a city
In this dance I'll know what to do
No left foot in a right shoe
On every current I must ride
Today I awoke looking out
From my eyes of a child.

Alison Cox

The Truth Never Dies

He wonders if there are too many now,
The writer, the poet, all trying to carve a niche.
Yet, the path remains open for those
Willing to tread the uncharted road,
To pursue the iniquities, the ever-increasing
Volatile world; the greed, the lies, corruption,
The deceit, and those who 'have', still searching,
Grasping, for more.

He smiles as the word 'Dada' comes to mind,
A word far removed from baby talk,
But a literary artistic group who have removed
Barriers from the establishment's approach to
The arts. A group he admires and can relate to;
Whose ideals he tries to uphold, to embrace
The pursuit of that dispossessed word:
The truth!

James Fraser

The Meadow

I dreamed I was a child again
A child of seven or eight.
I ran barefoot through flowery fields
Where tempting treasures wait
For roving, restless little girls
Beyond the garden gate.

There cowslips by the cartload danced
And daisies dazzling white,
With buttercups all gleaming gold
And full of brilliant light,
With trefoil, yellow rattle, vetch -
A dream of child delight.

A myriad orchids stood erect
Of intricate designs,
Some purple, scented, spotted, veined,
With little scribbled lines
Like marks on yellow-hammers' eggs
Or ancient, runic signs.

I ran agog from joy to joy
On pollen-dusted feet
And down the slope to lower ground
Where brook and meadow meet,
Through ragged robins, ladies' smocks
And stands of meadow-sweet.

The air was fresh, the brook was clear
In sparkling, limpid flow,
And life was light and lush and sweet
And leisurely and slow.
But jerked awake all this I found
Was fifty years ago.

Editha Russell

After The Wedding

The little church was empty now,
Guests to the reception gone.
Save for the two shadowy figures
Kneeling and quite alone.

'That brought back a memory or two, Bert,'
Said the lady
As silvery tears sped down her cheeks.
'Dear, living in this wonderful place
For all those years, months and weeks
Means that your tears are quite misplaced, Grace,
As our happiness was quite complete.

However, there was one small thing
Which marred our perfect life,
Just a little hitch,
My loving and faithful wife,
For we never did win that Dunmow Flitch!'

When this diatribe was over,
The two ghosts left the church,
Then promptly disappeared.

Shirley Jones

Cornwall

Oh yes, I am about to boast because I live by the coast,
Barbecues on the beach, it's all there within my reach,
The warmest region is where I dwell,
Lobster pots and crab shells,
Rugged cliffs and narrow streets,
Where farmers toil and crops they reap,
'Get on my lovers,' they call to their sheep,
Where the sun shines and the hills are steep,
'Orrite me bird?' the locals say,
Where pasties are made and large bales of hay,
Cornwall is home, and I'm here to stay,
Nowhere is better, to work, rest and play.

Julie Struggles

Nature's Night

Revealed by the moonlight on the forest floor,
Many scurrying paws as they leave their spoor.
Filtering light through the shadowy trees,
The pine-scented air wafts on the breeze
And silent owls fly over the moor.

One swoop and a vole is in a claw.
Untimely death, part of nature's law.
A creature seized with such ease,
Revealed by the moonlight.

Now the light streams through an old barn door,
The female owl with her chicks in the straw
Vole meat now used, their hunger to appease.
Torn to pieces with a pull and a squeeze,
Gone in a flash and they look for more,
Revealed by the moonlight.

Margaret Cutler

Tread Gentle Sheep Where Arrows Sped

I came to Battle Abbey on the day
An autumn sun lay warm upon the lea,
Where long ago King Harold, holding sway,
Was slain - confusion reigned - thanes turned to flee.
In fields that drop to distant groves
Sheep innocently munching in the sun
Would blink to learn how, in their droves,
French closed with Saxon till Duke William won.
The sands of Normandy still on their feet,
Whoever perished lie beneath the soil -
Quiet resting place a-tune with gentle bleat
Of sheep - so sweet a sound could never spoil
The calm unfolding to a distant haze,
Pierced through with leafy copses all ablaze.

Gloria Smith

Beauty And Beast

Fiery, flaming, brilliant crimson and red
Such a sight!
With shades of orangey-yellow in the sunshine
Oh! So bright!
A fragile flight of fancy blowing in the wind
Oh! So free
The poppy fields - a beautiful picture
For all of us to see.
No warning signs: *Keep Out, Stay Clear,*
Don't touch, Beware
Please open your eyes
To hidden dangers lurking there.
Their brightness and beauty
Now totally disappears
Weird fantasies, dark shadows
Bring unimaginable fears.
Addiction takes over
Your life out of control
Completely destroying body, mind
And even your soul.
So helplessly broken
Loved ones look on in despair
Hearts filled with sorrow
Their tears fall gently down
On your now empty chair.

Jean Arscott

The Seasons

The snow is softly falling
To some it is appealing
On a cold and frosty morning
It can be quite unfeeling.

But spring is round the corner
In colourful array
Each and every flower
Lifts its head to greet the day.

Then, the warmth of summer
When holidays abound
Soaking up the sunshine
Where it can be found.

Autumn, too, is lovely
With leaves of different hue.
Which is the nicest month of all?
I leave the choice to you.

Rose Broadbent

Lost Forever

The best lines to a poem
are the forgotten ones -
no pen or paper to hand
the fleeting words remain
a second then vanish
hoovered up in the dense
morass of verbal clouds
drifting out of reach and beyond
left only with the blank memory -
an amputation from what
was the perfect line to that
exact beginning of a thought.

Wendy Sullivan

Born Too Late

I was born too late for our history great
And apologise for living today,
For missing the Crimea, Mons and Korea,
Waterloo, Dunkirk and bloody Malplaquet.

I beg your forgiveness for being so vigorous
In not carrying my guilt while living
When so many they gave for a foreign grave
In the days of bloodshed and killing.

I'm sorry I live now and not at Lucknow
When the sepoys came looking for blood,
And forgive my remiss for having to miss
The hell of Passchendaele's mud.

Forgive me my age for my youth still pays
Its penance in a peace that has lasted,
And a conscience clear wants you to hear
From a generation not bombed or blasted.

So let's get this straight before it's too late
All you generations who think mine manqué
If war came again you'd find your young men
Just as brave in their marching away:

To fronts far from home for duties they own
Just as loyally as the generations lamented,
And die just the same in agony and pain,
The young people with lives you resented.

So do not berate those generations whose fate
Was to live when the great wars were done,
But think instead that this peace of the dead
Is our freedom for generations to come.

Peter Waverly

2009 - 21 Years

Forward Press, 21 years old
Million poets published
Anthologies galore
Thank you, Forward Press
You've published me several times
It's you where I started
A friend got me to send a poem in
Got published
Yippee, yippee, I thought, *I'm in print*
Then you continued to print my poems
I hope I will have many more in print
Anthologies, anthologies, my poems in print
Thank you, Forward Press
21 years, you're coming of age
The people love you
You showcase the British public's poems
You got me to be a poet
Peterborough is where you're based
Hail, hail, Forward Press
Many more years to come
Many more millions of poems published
Many more sent by me hopefully published
Keep up the excellent work
Excellent editors keep up the excellence
Many more years in Peterborough
Don't move, stay there Peterborough
Happy coming of age, Forward Press
21 years.

Michelle Knight

Hallam

Have you ever heard
Of the mighty Bess of Hardwick
Who built manors as fast as
She demolished her husbands?

Have you heard of Peveril
The old castle of the peak?
Its ruins still guarding from high
Mam Tor the trembling mountain.

Have you heard of Blue John
The cavern where Romans
Already valued and mined
This unique gem of a stone?

Have you ever heard of Dore
Where Mercia and Northumbria
After so much feuding
Decided to share peace?

Have you heard of Little John
Resting said the legend
In the green valley of Hope
Round the deep bend called the Surprise?

Have you seen in Robin Hood country
Nestling on craggy hills
Lonely farms, in winter
Islands lost in desolation?

Have you met these people
As hardy as the crops they grow
Faces carved like weathered rocks
Tenderly rescuing lambs in the snow?

When autumn dawns on the moors
Erica in blooms, silvern gossamer
Delicately holding the morning dew
Have you see these vast seas of coral?

Have you heard of this place
That was once called Hallam
Where history and beauty
Blend so naturally?

J C Chandenier

Othello (The Shopkeeper)

I have called him Othello
For so he seems,
Sturdy as a buffalo
With a welcoming beam.
How does he sense my mood
And perceive my sad thoughts?
As he stacks the tins of food
I feel playfully stalked.

Pocket-pens regimentally arranged
In his too-small blue smock
The jocund way he counts my change
Causes my smile to unlock.

'Thanking you, Miss, do call again'
(He eyeballs me over his glasses)
His domain was the African plain
But now his kingdom is molasses.

Helen Francis

A Bench At High Elms

I stand in the meadow where wild daisies grow
And birds sing their homage to the valley below

My head is well weathered, my back by sun browned
My feet firmly planted, secure on the ground

The old reminiscence here of happier days
And young mothers gossip while small children play

Fond lovers entwine here with soft words and sighs
I find their initials carved deep in my sides

A traveller will rest here, his pack causing pain
His staff strong and sturdy on Earth's sweet terrain

I serve here in silence, no recompense due
Through each changing season, to each year anew.

Mary Weber

Of Time

I am but a speck within the universe.
I am here and now. I've also been and gone.
I can bring much joy and help to everyone.
I can also bring much pain and sorrow.
So the path that I tread must be a careful one.

You are here amongst the pleasant landscape.
You are here to learn when all is done.
You must do it always your own way.
You must feel some rain and also sun.
So the path you tread must be a measured one.

We are here together for a reason.
We are here to undertake some special role.
We may never know until its finish.
We may never see our lives as whole.
So the path we tread must satisfy our soul.

Be all you are and live the good way.
Be all you can and seek the best.
Be all you wish and never worry.
Be content and be at rest.
So the path you tread will stand the test

Of time . . .

Christine Frederick

A Child's View Of Christmas

Mum took her little girl to see
A tableau - the Nativity.
The baby slept, and not a sound
Disturbed the peace and calm around
The newborn life.

'That must be Mary,' said the child,
Gazing at the mother mild.
'However could they bear to kill
Her lovely Son, who did God's will
And gave His life?'

'Two thousand years have passed since then,'
Her mother answered,' and yet when
We meet the greedy men of Earth
We wonder if His humble birth
Could save Man's life.'

'Yes, it can,' the children replied,
'Good people know that Jesus died
Teaching us to love each other.
That is why the Holy Mother
Gave Him His life.'

Maggie Tate

Lost Memories

As he sits and stares at me, does he comprehend,
Do those dear familiar eyes see me as a friend,
Does he know I need him so,
Does he understand,
Does he know I'm weeping as I take him by the hand?

He, my rock, my strength, my love,
Ever in control,
Sitting trembling, lost, bewildered,
Body without soul.

Surely if he sees my anguish,
He will ease my pain,
Just as he has always done so,
Time and time again.

As he sits and stares at me, does he comprehend?
Sadly no, he's said goodbye, my dear beloved friend.

I must start a new beginning, coping on my own,
But in my heart be sure of this, he never will be gone.

J Ross

Forty

For forty years I have been alive
Waiting for my wisdom to arrive.
I read the books and tried hard at school,
I bent and broke emotional rules.

I laughed a lot and cried even more,
I hammered for years upon closed doors.
I kicked some balls at an open goal,
I tried to break even and lost my soul.

Now I am forty and know little,
There are no happy starts or middles.
I cling to my family and friends
And hope there will be a happy end.

Bridie Glover

The Nine Ages Of Man (Life In The Fast Lane)

Brought up in emotionless sterility
In a respectable cocoon;
Wrought up in devotionless civility
Like some susceptible baboon.

The rota of teachers at my school
Wielded cruel bamboo rods to chasten me;
Their quota of speeches were a tool
Yielded to the shampoo gods of Masonry.

I left my school for a tertiary college
Was stoked and throttled by self-reliance;
Bereft, with a fool's cursory knowledge
I choked on bottled-up defiance.

One look at Vicki and I fell in love
Smitten by misplaced trust and fever;
She took the mickey that repelling dove
Bitten by distaste, lust and Shiva.

So through the trauma of divorce
Our vows were broken with finality;
I sat in a corner with remorse
Our rows a token of banality.

Here comes my latent nervous breakdown
NHS fee for a tranquillizer;
I hate the patent drugs I shake down
Some ECT and a glass of Tizer.

Been through the quagmire of mental illness
To dole dependency attuned;
Seen through the bonfire to inner stillness
My soul's ascendancy dragooned.

It brings me luck in my retirement
To push the mower and level your lawn;
Spreading the muck is your requirement
A fuchsia grower, the Devil for scorn.

In a home, a moist-eyed trolley dodger,
I leave my tea to go quite tepid;

I'm a gnome with hoisted Jolly Roger,
Before I'm finally decrepit.

Andrew Stephenson

Two Teddy Bears

Two teddy bears wait on an empty bed,
'When is he coming back?' they said,
'When will we see a golden head
Lying beside us upon the bed,
While we look on as prayers are said?'

Two teddy bears sit on a cover of blue,
'Where is the little boy we knew?
Eyes all mischief and hair askew,
Laughter that made us both laugh too,
We're lonely and don't know what to do.'

One old teddy has fur of brown,
He sits upon the eiderdown,
With spotted bow-tie like a clown,
One ear sticks up and one lies down,
But on his face he wears a frown.

The other bear has fur of blue,
With bow-tie of the self-same hue,
So proud and smart when he was new,
But now a nose stuck on with glue,
And he is sad and lonely too.

They wait while months turn into years,
Each harks a voice that neither hears,
And so their hopes turn into fears,
The room is locked and no one nears,
They never saw the mother's tears.

Two teddy bears grow dusty and old,
In an empty room alone and cold,
Where is the boy with curls of gold?
Where are the hands they used to hold?
What is the secret they haven't been told?

Ah, grown-up people are rarely wise
Enough to see sorrow in brown glass eyes,
Or know that heart and feeling lies
'Neath fabric fur and blue bow-ties,
And who would think a teddy cries?

A child would know because he shares
His world and thoughts with teddy bears;
A lone, neglected life is theirs,
He's gone forever and no one cares
For broken-hearted teddy bears!

Ailsa Keen

Eyeless In Gaza

Black smoke over Gaza
White smoke over the Vatican
Blood on the street and piazza
While I read *Flarepath* by Rattington
No one crosses the Rubicon

Oh, the blooded ones and the bloody fools
This folded reality between Arabs and Jews
With too many gods there's little room to move
And any god is missing when it's time to soothe
Though avaricious to reprove

In these turbulent times
Of dishevelled merit and discredited credit
Bland nightmare crimes
Which our cultures endure and inherit
Burying them and it

It only proves one thing, dear Bishop Berkley
The existence of wanton, feckless, reckless duty
And not that of God remarkably
Instead of a longed for deity and beauty
We recline resigned to futility

Richard Glaze

City Of My Dreams

Through the mists of time her beauty shines,
My city of dreaming spires sublime.
She is the fairest of all the shires,
The one of which I'll never tire.

Steeped in history, it's Oxford for which my mind is ever yearning,
This ancient seat of eternal learning.
The 21st century is making its mark,
Although there is an easy escape to one of her beautiful parks.

And maybe watch a game of cricket,
This, my friend, is just the ticket.

The botanical gardens are such a joy,
Punts on the river gently gliding by.
With sunlight glinting on ripples in their wake,
In a dream of 'Alice in Wonderland' it's so easy to partake.

The tradition of May Morning is a wonder to behold,
At a very early hour, choirboys with sweet voices
                              sing on Magdalen Tower.
Then Morris dancers entertain us with jingling bells
                       and the cracking of their sticks,
Usually accompanied by a jolly accordionist.

I was born and bred in Oxford and here I'll always stay,
I will never leave her and travel far away.

Val Bermingham

Summer

I've been invited to write a poem -
I'd love to write a poem!
I need a subject, a title!
Summer! I love the summer, favourite season.
My poem will be about summer!

Summer sky - summer sun - white clouds -
All different from the other seasons - warmer, hotter!
Holidays at the seaside, on the beach!
In the country - in a caravan!

Holidays abroad! Exciting! Cultures, people - different!
Different money, difficult! Food - good!
More travelling with going abroad - plane,
Eurostar?

Ideal! This poem for summer - all ideal!
The reality? Summer weather? Bad!
Makes summer holidays expensive!
Summer - the shortest season of them all -
Over far too quickly!

I believe there is an answer!
Eternity! Perfection! Life with God -
Permanent, not temporary!
Perhaps even permanent summer!

Rosalind Weaver

Our Day Out

Our mam took us out for a picnic
To the park to see the ducks on the lake.
She pushed the baby in a big swing pram,
Which carried all we needed to take.
On the way to the park we stopped at the shop
To return empty bottles for pennies,
And to our delight, we got just enough
To buy a big bottle of pop.
This now went into the pram,
Along with the sandwiches made of jam.
We arrived at the park and sat on a rug
Laid out on the grass by Mam.
Then we all fed the ducks
With left over bits of crusts and crumbs of bread.

Mam was relaxing after feeding the baby,
Who now was asleep in the pram.
Then all at once came a shout of,
'Mam, our John's fallen into the lake.'
Up got Mother and in a flash,
She went into the lake as she was.
Though the lake was not very deep,
The water came up to her waist,
And she grabbed young John,
Pulling him out with very great haste.

By then there was a crowd of people around,
Unable to take it all in.
With mouths wide open and children screaming,
'Look, he went for a swim.'
Mam scolded the boy, then she hugged him with joy
And undressed him under the trees.
He said he stared at the water,
And it seemed to say, 'Come on in.'

By now John was wrapped in the tartan rug
And sitting in the bottom of the pram.
'What an awful ending to our day out,' said Mam,
As she wiped the drips from her chin.
We all had to hurry to keep up her pace,
As she sneezed and complained to us all the way home.

'Not a man in sight to help my plight,
Typical, don't you think?'
Who knows what your dadda will say . . . What a day!'
Then she gave us a wink.

Dylis M Letchford

Spring To Life

Shy snowdrops, bright harbingers of spring,
retire with grace, their glory on the wane.
Migrant cuckoo on the wing,
brazen daffs shine forth again
when they aspire to match the sun
promise that spring has now begun.

The annual show will soon unfold
the greatest show there is around,
when nature, unfettered from the cold,
begins to spring from latent ground,
clothing field and woodland floor
in vibrant green, alive once more.

Springing up in mass profusion
bluebells stretch like bluest ocean
through copse and meadow in sweet collusion.
Shimmering as a sea in motion
thro' Burroughs Wood, for all to see
spring's lavish show - what's more, it's free!

Horace Gamble

Cosmic Order

You speak of a place

where stars
are tea lights
to crossed paths -

where memories
store lives . . .
past loves . . .

where dreams
are footprints
impressed on sand

and sea -
as far as the eye
sees the journey

without beginning,
its course
without end.

Is this our gift -
the cord that ties
north and south . . .
miles of land
and psychometry
of time?

We speak of a place . . .

seek signs.
Thoughts pass
dark hours

between us.
Midnight
enters and leaves.

Candice Morgan

The Moon Looks Down

The pale moon looks down
as the human race slowly tears itself apart.
Through the mustard sky she observes
the stinking streets overflowing with garbage.

What will they do next? she thinks.
They came and walked on me once,
but when they saw that they couldn't exploit me
they left and didn't come back.

After numerous experiments and tests
plus a little promenade or two, they deposited
a peculiar box and a flag . . .
but I got rid of them.

On the return journey
one of the crew became religious:
seeing the Earth from another perspective
he decided it was proof enough.

He went home and gave lectures,
this Earthman: about God and the Great Achievement.
Because they're not happy, you see, unless
they find an explanation for everything.

Yet curiously, despite their efforts,
and the example of their ancients, who mapped the skies
while remaining on the ground
and discouraged the worship of false idols

they still haven't learned
that there is only us: the planet and the stars.
Awesome and enormously relevant . . .
floating around mysteriously.

John Short

Dove

The bird had been trapped
hovering in my chest
since I was nine,
when war broke out.

Pecking endlessly at my insides
when I went to bed hungry,
in the cold, damp grave
of the air raid shelter.

Fluttering helpless against
the bars of my ribcage,
at the sky-filled humming
of the German Luftwaffe.

Piercing my ears with its cries,
at the bonfire smell
and the screeching
of the whistling bombs.

Beating its wings against my heart
at the sight of the rubble,
of what once had been
my granny's house.

Scratching my throat raw
at images of torpedoed ships
burning planes,
and dead, neglected soldiers.

Now the bird was free:
I opened my mouth, out it flew,
spreading soft white wings,
soaring upward into the quiet blue sky.

Past red, white and blue bunting,
jelly and custard street party din.
Two women leaned over me,
'Eat up, there's a love

The war is over. Just think
she is nearly fifteen,
doesn't eat enough
To keep a bird alive!'

Irene Ison

Rain Or Shine?

I wish I were a raindrop,
I'd fall down from the sky;
I'd help grow food to feed you
I'd stop the rivers running dry.
I'd let the sunshine warm me
Take me back into the sky.
I wish I were a raindrop
So I never had to die.

I wish I were a sunbeam,
Burning through the sky,
I could cause the grass to grow
Or could cause so much to die.
I can burn the ground you stand on
I can dry away the sea.
And when my time is over
All life will burn with me.

Becky Murphy

Great Britain

Great Britain, great class divide
Who or what your father is and does
Can determine how you'll survive
It's a shabby society, that's structured by class
One half on the fat of the land
The other on the bones of their arse
Privileged, self indulgent, pompous and vain
A big nose to look down and feel no shame

There's nothing great about Britain
Unless you're climbing that tree
She doesn't look quite so good, when you're down on one knee.

Anne Stead

Dual Identities

In fuel-tainted air a child city-bred
Cosseted by parents, treasured and well fed
Fast food junkie indulgence her birthright
Clutching old teddy she whispers goodnight
Free from fears under quilted bedspread
Sweet dreams drifting into her sleepy head.

In a barren desert her counterpart lies
On a mattress of soil under moonlit skies
Where every three seconds another child dies.
Confused and alone, no tears left to cry
On trembling lips a brief prayer fades
Aching for the parents claimed by AIDS.

Diverse cultures - paucity v plenty.
Black skeletal form draped in bright kente
Schooled in the beauty of lonely liberty.
Designer jeans clothe western puberty
Her world geared to high technology.
Both children victims of ideology.

Black and white sisters part of a mystery
Woven by God at the dawning of history
Dealt different cards in life's lottery
Hope's seeds planted in twenty-first century
As Western youth shake mists of lethargy
For Third World poverty demanding apology.

Kathleen Potter

On This Day

Today is the day if you look high into the air,
you can see your memories passing by, focus hard on that clear blue sky.
As you look upon that sky above, is that a dove flying above?
Look again, let your mind drift free,
for it's a pair of lovebirds that you can see.
They soar and sail as they swoop then climb,
just as your hearts did once upon a time.
Let your mind drift back to days gone by
when a handsome young man came into your life.
Sweeping you off your feet, he made you laugh, he made you cry.

You shared your dreams, they didn't all come true,
young hearts together with the world at your feet,
what would life have in store for you?
The life you shared was full of love, tenderness, hopes and dreams,
sometimes good, sometimes not,
but all in all a fulfilling and happy life.
He loved you then, he loves you now.
Although not together you know somehow, now alone,
 with your wonderful memories of times shared together
and the intimate moments that will never leave.

Of a life rich, not with wealth, but with a treasure of love
and affection that still lingers on.
So on this day, look back at your memories, your triumphs,
your family and friends, yet always remember . . .
Whilst the memories are alive you're never alone.

M James

Shore Leave

We'd been at sea thirty days, maybe more.
We've brushed and we've polished and ready for shore.
Primed for the liquor we'll soon consume.
Ready for the scent of cheap perfume.

Smoke-filled bars and grimacing bawds,
Asking much more than we can afford.
But we'll pay for the girls that we've engaged.
Strains of abstinence soon assuaged.

Light-headed now but the drink tastes good.
Song and dance while we're in the mood.
Girls become hazy, noises unclear.
Just for a little I'll stick to the beer.
And then all of a sudden, alone with a girl.
A shabby apartment, my head in a whirl.
A short burst of passion and soon fast asleep.
Dreamless and dark far, far in the deep.

And then comes the morning and slow to awake.
The girl is not with me, was it all a mistake?
I checked with my money, but all was secure.
It could not be surely, alone my allure?
I remembered but little of the night just gone by,
Except that the looks of the girl caught my eye.
Then during the revels we must have been drawn,
And remained then together till today's early dawn.

Dressed now and back to the ship I must go.
Unsure of the tide. Which the ebb, which the flow?
I must be on time, my home lies in water.
My worldly possessions, the things that I treasure.

Soon we'll be sailing back into the brine.
The sea that scarce changes through aeons of time.
We had our brief time in the lively old port.
The drinking, the dancing, the passionate sport.

We may be at sea thirty days, maybe more,
But some day and some time, we're again on the shore.

Cyril Joyce

We Should Say 'I Love You'

What are the words we rarely say, the words that mean so much?
'I love you.'
These words are rarely said, yet these words mean so much,
We should say them to one another, to the ones we care about,
But as we grow, we find it hard to show the love that's in our hearts,
So we let it go because we know they know just how we feel.

But what if we're wrong and they just don't know,
Just what we really think?
Would it hurt for us to say *'I love you'* and I really care,
It's rarely spoken, it's rarely said to the ones we love so much,
These three little words make a difference, so why do we shy away?

To hear *'I love you'* means so much, it means that we are special,
It means that someone cares for us,
It means we aren't alone, no matter where we are,
We tell our babies we love them daily, we tell our children too,
But when we reach that certain age we forget to say it then,

We forget to tell each other, as we know we should,
As for parents, siblings, children and loved ones too,
We all forget they need to know.
So just think back to when you last said, *'I love you'*
The worlds that mean so much.

Think back, when did you last say, *'I love you'* to someone
That is close?
Can you remember, I think you may not,
It's not so hard and would mean so much,
So to our parents, siblings, children and to our loved ones too,
To all we hold so dear,
Just say to them, *I love you'* and make it very clear

For one day, we know not when, we may not be able to
What then? It is too late, it's with regret and sadness too,
We'll wish we had,
Whilst looking back, whilst feeling sad,
We'll wish we'd said, *'I love you.'*

Michael James

Cumbria

There's nobody could choose a more delightful county,
where nature's precious garment is proudly displayed:
An exhibition of a frosty morning, that's adorned with pearly dew,
and brightly glistens in the cool, fresh, languid air . . .
There's mountains streams and river flow - from high above the hills, as fluffy
clouds drift over the Lakeland fells . . .
Roads are so much quieter, the sun has almost risen,
and the bird's song carries down a Heavenly stair . . .

Salt air mingles with a zephyr, from where lies an illustrious halcyon sea, a place
where seaweed gathers on golden sand . . .
There flotsam and jetsam rest, as seashells lie bejewelled,
while pebbles shine like starlight in the sky . . .
Boats ride at silent anchor; town houses awaken from their sleep,
as the sound of traffic moves to places across the land . . .

Now the sun looks so delightful, meadows carry a Heavenly hue,
while ivy embraces monastic turrets in a sunlight beam . . .
How verdant stand the leafy trees, around a once, proud, fractured
castle, where the silence wearily allows it peace and calm -
Diminishing mute shadows point to further historic views . . .
where sculpture, art and architecture can be seen . . .

A nearby town has come alive, there's the sound of shoppers
in the air, where stores display their produce for all to see-
There's a variety of handmade goods, and their quality looks just fine,
while their prices encourage everyone to spend.
Supermarkets are on hand, though some people prefer the little shop, where here-
folks' pleasantries and time are given free!

Thomas Ian Graham

Infinity

Looking for waters that run so cold,
Softly falling upon rocks of gold.

Waiting for fires that burn so bright,
Leaving only ashes in the moon's silvery light.

Carried away across golden sands,
To a secret valley in some far and distant land.

Searching for shadows upon the horizon,
But the images seen bear no resemblance.

This world is a pearl with a shiny exterior,
As the sun glides down, we feel small and inferior.

Thousands of souls drifting gently on clouds,
Beyond prisms of light, beyond echoes of sound.

Precious moments swept away with a
                diminishing wind, whose whispers say:

'The past has no ending,
The future no beginning.'
The present never goes away, not even for a day.
Eternally burning, always here to stay.

Kafi McCall

Unnamed

A quiet, docile, undemanding girl,
Of modest talents and of furtive bloom:
Who would have thought that eighteen years would see
Her silence sealed forever in the tomb;
Or that her insignificance would be
Distinguished by death's dreadful dignity.

Carole T O'Driscoll

Teach Us

Teach us to number our days,
These days which pass in crazy confusion,
These hours which are like moments,
These weeks which rush into oblivion,
These years which, too soon, are only memories,
Restrain us - teach us to number our days.

You, who art infinite and everlasting,
We, who are finite and fleeting,
You, who are strong, infallible and wise,
We, who are feeble, unstable and insecure,
You who created us and understand us -
Remember us- teach us to number our days.

Life is like a rushing river - out of control
Constantly seeking but not finding -
- Desiring but not being satisfied
- Striving but not being fulfilled
- Struggling to prove ourselves but never succeeding
Reclaim us, teach us to number our days.

Stop us in our tracks and remind us
Life has direction, meaning and purpose -
Only if we submit to, and serve our Creator,
Our times are in Your hands -
So, free us from our struggles and give us contentment
Renew us - teach us to number our days.

Give us peace in resting and trusting,
Give us purpose in serving,
Give us contentment in believing,
Fill the void with Your presence -
Come and rescue this perishing race,
Reach us - teach us to number our days.

Show us that in trusting we will find rest,
In repentance we will find forgiveness,
In believing we will find hope.
Show us the reason for our existence -
Give us the vision of eternity -

With You - endless delight -
Without You - everlasting despair.
Redeem us - teach us to number our days
And therein find *wisdom* and *peace!*

Hazel J E McMinn

Not Nearly Enough

If thou loved me, thou would tell me so,
I do love thee, why, I shall shout it so.
When will it ever be enough?
Too much is never enough but
Sometimes
Less is more
I'm sure though
Enough is enough
Have I said too much?
Not nearly enough so
Speak no more now
You could never say it right.
You're right,
I was wrong in trying
Wrong in doing
Two, which don't make a right.
Say what?
If thou loved me thou would simply say it so,
I do love thee; just give me a chance though.

Shelley Farr

Rumbling Bridge

Rumbling through the gorge;
Reverberating!
Cascading!
A frightening, terrible sound,
this rage of fluid anger,
of savage, torrid waters
rampaging through the hills.
Each relentless, angry drop
pounds the ancient stones;
in contention for its strength.

Its deafening roar, bears witness
as foaming, churning liquid
plummets to its death:
swirling in depression
at the foot of a rumbling bridge.
Historic bridge, well christened;
reflecting an awesome sight
as cracked and beaten boulders,
are pummelled and pounded smooth
and moulded, beaten granite
is carved in the image of rage.

Whilst tree roots snapped and torn
with the fierceness of its might.
serve to remind mere humans
of their puny, fragile state.

Felicity M Greenfields

25th June 2009

A legend died today
But *The* Legend was born
Your music, your moves are gone
But will live forever
On tape, vinyl and mobile phone.
Your voice so pure, even as a lad
And then came the feet -
Your moves drove us mad.
History shows every genius has a flaw
But those around you should have done more
To nurture and protect
The person you wanted to forget -

Your lovely face altered and scarred
The man so publicly, bizarrely marred
Trying to hide the fear you felt inside -
Perhaps you had already died.

And now that you are gone
The press and hangers-on
Will not let you rest.

You were the best
And no matter what they say
It's true -
A legend died today.

J Little

Life's Walk

Along this path I go,
where it leads to, no one knows,
and so, this path I walk;
night and day, long or short: who can say?
But still I walk this way,
I have no choice; night or day.
Sometimes a seat I'll find
and rest a little while; then on my way again,
with strength to face new trials.

The tide is turning now,
I watch it from on high;
but cannot reach the shore
and only watch and cry.
But still this path I walk
And wonder where it goes;
Time will surely tell,
as years fade and grow.

Rosalind B Meadows

Washington DC

Pale stone buildings in classical style
Constructed neatly in rows, mile upon mile,
From Capital Hill where the Senate meets
To cherry tree blossoms like snow in the streets.
A science museum with artefacts from space
An astronaut's suit from the first moon race,
The Potomac River winding all through the city
Past flowerbeds and woodland, elegant and pretty.
Lincoln's Memorial impressive in size
Founding Father and President, solemn and wise,
Union Station with gigantic shopping hall
Silver bullet trains, hear the shrill whistle call.
And oh, the White House with neat gardens and park
USA capital - Washington - its power and its heart.

Jean Mackenzie

Rare Book

How many hands have held you,
Sitting by the fireplace?
How many hands have touched you,
On your lovely face?
How many eyes read you,
And talk of what you say?
You taught them all a thing or two,
You gave them all a better view,
A start in life all brand new,
Intelligence for university,
To teach young and old,
Lots of stories to be told,
I'm pleased to have held you
In my hands and heart.
You're very old and frail.
Old book, no sale.

Isabel Buchanan

The Story Of The Lonely Stray . . . The End

Brown were the eyes of the friend I remember,
Faithful, loving and true,
Glad we shared life in June and December,
Happy as long as it was we two.
Many the journeys and walks together,
Days full of wonder, evenings of charm.
Down on the seashore, and through the bright heather,
Happiest of all when we shared the wood's charm.
These are the memories I always will treasure,
Brown eyes will not look into mine anymore,
But I will give thanks for the finest dog ever,
Knowing no other his place will restore.
Some people have never known the love of a dog,
To have had him was far beyond words,
To have loved and lost him, was better by far,
Than him not being loved at all.

Doreen Brennan

New York City

Another day to work-wise over the Manhattan skies
Normality reigns throughout traffic lanes.
Business as usual on city-life street
With the sun smiling down to say its good morning.

Out of bed, people rise under Manhattan skies.
Doors open in stores and coffee shop floors.
Newspaper vendors on sidewalk ways. All part of life in the city.

No one can surmise how it felt in the Manhattan skies
As near to the sun, terror had just begun.
A day that shook the world and changed life in the city forever.

Some said their goodbyes over the Manhattan skies,
With a 'love you' message, remaining ever precious.
All in one day, Man destroyed Man and left millions wondering, why?

The city, it cries below Manhattan skies:
Tears flow for everyone. Life's infinite journey's just begun.
People shocked to the core of their very being.

New York lies under Manhattan skies.
Abnormality came, to change its name.
Even the sun was blinded by the dust as it tried to hug the brave,
The loved and the shadows of humanity.

> The city *will* rise to meet Manhattan skies
> And the sun *will smile again.*

Katebell

The Price We Have To Pay

We used to think we were ten out of ten
We've gone so low we've got to think again
My girl

You believe: we can start all over
But all we can do is grow older
My girl

Don't say: we've things to talk about
When we continue to scream and shout
My girl

You insist: it's going to be alright
But hope is another excuse for another hopeless fight
My girl

You're crying crocodile tears now
It didn't take you long to find out how
My girl

You had me wrapped 'round your fingertips
I'm going to miss the kiss from your bittersweet lips
My girl

Go away, stay, go away, stay
I was so confused I just didn't know what to say
Go away, stay away, go away, stay away
We have to part as it's the price we have to pay.

Luis Dalmedo

The Gift Of Love

Some may say that love is overrated,
Some say love is hard to find and easy to lose

Even I believed this true till the day you came

'Some say' love is all about family and friends
But I think love is for all to enjoy

Love is a gift to be given freely to the ones you love

Some may say that love is overrated
'Some say' love is like death
Even I believed it to be true
Until the day we came face to face

Love is a gift from Heaven, and so are you
. . . Love is the day you came into my life,
And the love we shared will last me a lifetime

Some may say love is overrated
But I believe love is a gift, the gift you gave to me.

PS: I hope one day I will be able to share my life with you.

St Catherine Henville

The Enchanted Wood

Kind ghosts, smiling at me
wherever I go . . .
among leaves of memory

'Keep it safe, the old tree'
they whisper low,
kind ghosts smiling at me

Close friends and family,
all springtime on show
among leaves of memory

On a nature trail to eternity
where love's seeds grow,
kind ghosts smiling at me

If the self is its own enemy,
let its colours show
among leaves of memory

Keeping such company,
the poet I would be;
kind ghosts smiling at me
among leaves of memory.

Roger Taber

Think Of Me

Think of me in the tunnel long
Think of me and make me strong
Strong to walk this dark, dark way
Without so much as a sunbeam's ray.

Think of me and give me hope
Just a spark to help me cope
At this time, so black and bleak
A light, a light is all I seek.

I am crying to God and you
Tell me, tell me, what I must do,
Show me the way that I must know
To make the tunnel my friend
And not my foe.

Dear friend of mine, all I can say
I hold you close and pray and pray
That God, our Father in His love
Will give you strength His power to prove
That, oh so soon, you will see
A very close affinity, in all you are and seek to be
Revived, restored, renewed and free.

Mabel Dickinson

The Joyful Heart

Shrieks of laughter, cries of joy
Come from every girl and boy.
Happiness is in the air,
Tumbling down around her chair.
Swinging high and swinging low,
Hear the children as they go
Higher up and higher still,
As of life they drink their fill.
She can't see them but she hears,
Look now and you will see the tears
As she recalls that far-off day
She could do the same as they.
Smiles now as her mind recaptures
Long ago, childhood raptures.
Little do the children know
The wondrous gift they bestow,
For - comes her time to depart,
She'll leave with a joyful heart.

Daphne Lodge

My Mother's Love

Someone touched my hand last night, a light and gentle touch.
They touched my soul then whispered that they loved me very much.
Someone's presence, someone near, I felt the warmth around.
Yet nothing stirred - except my heart - not the slightest sound.

Someone's taking care of me along my life's pathway.
Someone very special, very dear in every way.
Someone helps me through the times when I need a helping hand.
Someone tells me how to cope with things I cannot understand.

Someone who's left this Earthly space, someone I miss so much.
Yet someone's still so very close - so close they almost touch.
I can feel the love and the strength of the one I knew so long.
It powers through each day I live - a feeling - oh, so strong.

Someone's love so pure and sweet it's really like no other.
A special bond, a special love, given only from a mother.
I miss my mum and, most of all, her loving and her giving.
The one who gave me my life and the reason for my being.

Patricia Marland

Feud

A lifetime of regret results from spite -
for words, once uttered, cannot be withdrawn.
Their poison seeps into the very soul
of those alive (and even those unborn).

The time to put things right has slipped away -
as pride withholds the move to make amends.
Now silence reigns and hatred comes to stay,
instead of warmth between two loving friends.

The years go by, while others join the fray -
and battle-lines have now become entrenched.
The story, handed down, infects them all;
their eyes stay closed and hands meet fists still clenched.

Ellen Green Ashley

Mist On The Meadow, The Sun On The Stream

How I remember days long ago,
Everyone happy, but no place to go -
Never much money and not much to spare,
But what we had then, happy to share.

These were the old days, happier then.
We laughed together down in the glen.
How I remember of how life can seem,
Mist on the meadow
The sun on the stream.

Folk stopped to listen, took time to talk.
Very few cars then, just had to walk.
Everyone happy, smiling all day,
Happy contented, as they went on their way.
These were the old days, happier then,
We laughed together down in the glen,
How I remember of how life can seem,
Mist on the meadow
The sun on the stream
Mist on the meadow
Or was it a dream?

Betty Miller-Arnold

How Long Will I Love Thee?

How long will I love thee?
As long as the stars shine in the sky at night
How long will I love thee?
As long as the rain falls on the land
And I can hold it in my hand
How long will I love thee?
Till the seas no longer ebb and flow
Till the gales and winds no longer blow
Till the moon no longer waxes and wanes
And the seasons no longer change
Till the world is no more
I will love thee.

Mary Loader

A GM Day

What if I could,
If just for one day,
Genetically modify
Everything my way?

Don't care so much
For diamonds and gold
Care a lot more
For those who are old!
For all of those then,
Let me make them a day
Brimful with youth
And the sweetness of May.
For all those at war
There is a simple solution,
I would fill all their hearts
With a peace revolution.
For all those we've lost
I would find us a way
To have them return
For just one more day.
All pain and illness
Of course would be gone
Cures would be found
The nano before dawn.
For those that I love
I won't change a thing
I couldn't make better
All that they bring.
On this one day
Yet to become
My desk will be tidy
Every job done.
Paperwork lying
In neat little piles
All the right words
In all the right files.

And so to bed early
To be up with the dawn
For that day when it starts
Will so quickly be gone.

Vivienne Anderson

Faces Of Dementia

What would I see if I looked through your eyes?
A world with children playing in the street,
Endearing puppies begging at your feet,
Imaginary people that you greet
When, really, you address an empty seat.

How would it feel to be inside your mind?
Elusive strands of thought emerge, then twist
To float enticingly in clouded mist.
You fight to grasp them back, in vain resist
Their passing. Then they dissipate, dismissed.

How would I cope if I lived in your world?
A muddled maze of yesteryear, beset
With troubled ramblings riddled with regret.
You're living in a nightmare landscape, yet
When morning comes you're likely to forget.

We'll treasure, then, these special lucid times
When precious shafts of sunlight filter through;
Grey clouds depart and thought is clear and true,
Sweet memories awake, revive anew
The person I still recognise as you.

Rosemary Williams

The Great British Summer

It's the end of the summer, I thought to myself
As the wind blew the heads off my flowers
The bullets of rain on the conservatory roof
Had been trying to get in for hours.

There was a chill in the air and we put on the light
As the autumn was rearing its head
Then I woke up today to a wonderful sight
We've an Indian summer instead.

As the heat of the day pushed the autumn away,
The shorts and the T-shirt went on
The suncream came out as we all fell about
As the rays of the sun shone and shone.

It's typical though now the kids are at school
In their classrooms they're having to be
No more running around now they've all gone to ground
Instead of getting some vitamin D.

All summer long the wet weather went on
Were we never to see some fine weather?
If you happened to wait and then holidayed late
You'd have felt that you were ever so clever

But it's all down to chance not worth even a glance
At the forecast you see on the telly
You will have a good time if you're always resigned
To taking your brolly and wellies.

Audrey Harman

Pilgrimage

Convey us in your silver car, dear Father!
O lead us, Heavenly Father; in Thy care:
With parting prayers and holy water shield us
Thence, o'er moor and fen the open highway there.
There, where - in a vision to Richeldis[1] - came,
The Virgin Mary, holy Mother fair;
Enshrinéd was her image and restoréd
By Hope Patten[2] - in the twenties - vicar there.

Alas, we cannot stop to pay a visit
Where lie the mouldering bones of Aragon[3],
We can but merely glimpse afar its splendour,
This most glorious portal in all Christendom[4].
A ride away from Eliot's Little Gidding[5],
The building was begun in eleven eighteen
With Benedictine medieval precincts;
More - within - a painted ceiling can be seen!

The Norman nave of this - St Peter's Minster
We needs must view - imbibe - some other day;
Just now, we make our comfort stop McDonald's,
There - proceed to eat packed lunches; then - away
To a shrine that's not *Kathedra* like the Boro';
Our Lady's Holy England's Nazareth[6],
Where pilgrims by the score still flock to honour
Mary, and her part in life surpassing Death.

Andrew Newman Pellow
Footnotes
Lady Richeldis [1] - inhabitant of the Manor of Walsingham,
Norfolk in the reign of Edward the Confessor.

Fr Hope Patten [2] was Vicar of Walsingham from 1921-1958.
Katherine of Aragon [3] Henry VIII promised she should be remembered by 'one of
the goodliest monuments in Christendom'.

The West front of Peterborough Cathedral 4 is thus described.

T S Eliot 5 (1888-1965). Little Gidding was celebrated by him in one of his 'Four
Quartets'.

The shrine of Our Lady of Walsingham 6 is known all over Europe as 'England's
Nazareth'.

To Those Figures On The Ground

One 6th August morning,
In Doncaster town centre, I saw
That several chalk figures had strangely appeared.
They made me puzzle
About who would want to draw
Such pictures on the pavement, vivid and weird,
Like murder victims,
Contours of evidence
That compelled my curious eyes
To explain to the brain
Their mysterious presence,
What particular purpose they personalize.
When at work, I thought
No more about why
Those intriguing outlines had been portrayed so;
And later that evening,
On returning by,
No tantalising trace was left on show.
At night, in the pub,
I was told that it
Was the anniversary today
Of when that horror happened,
Hiroshima being hit
By an atomic bomb dropped from the Enola Gay,
That B-29
Sent without pity
To demoralise, devastate and render dread,
Cause maximum damage
All over the city,
With 150,000 wounded or dead;
And then Nagasaki,
The next target attacked,
Suffered a similarly lethal blast,
Just three days later,
In a frightening act
Of desperate conflict, soon destined not to last.
This is why someone
Had shown emotion from the heart
And publicly left those poignant images,
A haunting reminder

In symbolic art
That conveys how atrocity's human damage is
Agonised by sacrifice
And absolute awe,
For mortal core-memory must never be allowed
Ever to forget,
In this terrible war,
The nuclear carnage of a mushrooming cloud.

David Coates

If Only . . .

If only they knew that a fruitless life
Could be changed by the power of prayer.
That the urge to destroy could be stopped
If they knew that God was there.

If only they knew that wars could cease
That love and peace could prevail,
If they heeded God's word to love each other
And know God's word wouldn't fail.

If only they knew that to give one's love
If in God's word they believed,
Would reap its own special rewards,
For to give, is to receive.

If only they knew how sad God is
When He sees his world destroyed,
By greed and hate, then hopefully;
Such things they would avoid.

If only they knew, if they faced their fears
In whatever may betide,
Of the comfort they would feel to know,
That God was by their side.

Mavis Wright

Key Of Success

So Forward Press, your year has come
Just writing lots of rhymes for fun
You now have a key to your success
Twenty-one years of going to press

I hope I have helped some of the way
Hence this little rhyme from me today
Lots of people share your joy
Even my little friend, a ten-year-old boy

All these verses we do write
Just make us happy day and night
And when we get the books to read
Once again we know how to succeed

So congratulations to you all
Just carry on and have a ball!

Pam Chappell

Remission

Bright cherry breast nipples
Dimpled in the coming dawn
Of her desires!
Waiting for her love
On the bright light morn
She touches the skin - so soft
The eruption of desires to explore
A phoenix rising from the ashes
Memory scorched - seared - red-hot
Heliotrope heavy lidded eyes -
Spins the pencil line across the dent
Of her eyeball
Pumps Rouge Absolute on her swollen, waiting lips
Wraps the satin gown stiff with tears
Tight to her heart now
Daisy petals on the floor - one, two, three
He loved me once didn't he?

Carol Palmer-Ayres

Mothers

(Dedicated to Mum)

Our mum's best in the world
Don't you agree?
Well they are to you and me
They give us birth, we give them mirth
With our little antics
And as a child we're so meek and mild
But we, in later life, can give them pain
Yes, we are to blame
But let us be good for motherhood
For all the mothers in the world
Are the best, don't you agree
To you and me?

Robert Walker

To Audrey Hepburn

Like an angel on our silver screen,
You've such glamour, uniquely serene.
All the drama in your lovely face,
And a dancer's remarkable grace.
So much love from your fans you earned,
Plus the Oscar, for which you yearned.

'My Fair Lady's' stern Higgins you charm,
Dressed exquisitely, you take his arm.
You are zany and playful and jolly,
As dear 'Breakfast at Tiffany's' Holly!
Helping UNICEF you used your art,
Hope and joy and resolve to impart,
With your natural warmth - from the heart.

Marion Whistle

Crime

What right have these bullying monsters
To mug, hurt and maim,
To ruin people's lives
So they can never be the same?
These people whom they mug,
They take away their pride,
They are too frightened to go out,
And feel just as bad inside,
Too afraid to answer the door
When people come calling,
A prisoner in their own home,
Is really so appalling.
What happens to these thugs,
If and when they are caught?
A few months in jail,
For all the heartaches they have brought,
Then they are set free, to start all over again
Whereas the victims are left
To suffer the hurt, worry and pain.
It's a sad fact, but true,
The thug becomes the free,
Whilst the victim is the prisoner,
This should never ever be!

B M Wood

Darling

Darling, I love you
You are so divine
I think a lot of you
Cos you are mine
When I'm away from you
I really do pine
Eventually I'll be with you
And things will be fine.

Theresa Hartley-Mace

Twenty One

Twenty-one is an important stage
In having reached the coming of age.
Also twenty-one in days of yore
Was when you gained the key of the door
And parental consent was no longer required
In marrying the person one so desired.
Twenty-one is a royal gun salute
In paying honour as a worthy tribute.
Twenty-one is also a card game
Better known by its French name!
In the periodic table
Scandium has the twenty-one label.
Now we have reached the twenty-first century
We must 'press forward' ever hopefully!

Letitia Lawrence

In Your Dreams

Tonight, I come to you . . .
in your dreams,
whispering softly
through your sleeping limbs
as I lead you through the
vacuum of space,
slipping, sliding, swimming and swirling
in the vast blackness
of cosmic endlessness,
one in blissful emptiness,
iridescent, glowing,
resembling the morning star
at the break of dawn.
Truly we love
when we fly free.

Jacqueline Zacharias

Autumn

Sadly, softly, fall the leaves
Passing one another by
Under a grey and thoughtful sky;
Pausing in the smoky air,
They don't care . . .
But I do . . . in this reverie,
This time of well-worn memory
I see again the avenue,
All broad and tree-lined; two by two
The decent houses lie in wait
And then the room . . . and you.
Just once I look, then, like a book
I shut you in-between the leaves
And put you back, high on the shelf . . .
And hate myself.

Una Davies

A Time Of Grieving

The quietness covers me like a shroud,
I listen for your voice to call my name aloud,
The pathway forward is dim, I scarce can see,
I long for the warmth of your body next to me.

In the darkness of the night, my hand reaches out for you,
To press my fingers to your lips, like you used to do.
I hold my aching body, from deep within I cry,
My love you slipped away from me, no time to say goodbye.

Lost in a sea of faces, not feeling arms that entwine,
Around my weary body, I float in space and time,
Drowning in words of comfort, praying for strength to get through,
The endless days and lonely nights, I weep, my love, for you.

There is a time of grieving when nought can ease the pain
Of losing someone that you loved, wanting them back again.
Time passes slowly, life's threads picked up anew,
Sweet memories stay until that day, my love I'll come to you.

June Goodwin

Is This The World That God Made?

'Is this the world that God made?'
Cried the angels in despair
As they viewed the devastation
From their stations in the air

Children cry in hunger
As the rebels power gain
There are disputes, there is chaos
Devastation in their train

There is warfare, there is hatred
There is needless loss of life
When will men learn to reason
There is nothing gained by strife?

When God foresaw the universe
It was with an eye of pride
A place of peace and plenty
That no man could deride

But greed and gain and power
Brought down the rule of law
And Man completely vandalised
The world the Almighty saw

Is there no end to chaos
Is content beyond reprieve
Can we gain again our dignity
And love and joy conceive?

Come, Mankind, destroy your weapons
And make a solemn vow
No more to raise corruption
Bring in Utopia here and now.

A Aston

Twenty-One This Year

Twenty-one this year,
Twenty-one this year,
Forward Press really deserves
A hearty, great big cheer.

Poets have seen their work
Published by this Press.
Over one million poems
Certainly not one less.

All types of subjects
From all kinds of men
Have all been written
With paper and pen.

Let's get together
And write a few more
So we can record
A wonderful score.

One million verses
By two thousand and nine
Will surely be doubled
If we all write a line.

Cynthia Dixon

Double Celebration

Life has a funny way
Of having its say.
You work hard for a living
And do a lot of giving.
It drags you down,
Down and down.
Something always brings you back up.
Let's raise a cup,
To your 21st and my 40th birthday,
That day we will have our say.

Joan Helen Grant

The Boy And His Pony

He's off on his pony,
    Off up the hill.
Breeze rushing by
    All adds to the thrill.
He's free as a bird,
    Just sat on his back,
Love and affection,
    They neither do lack.
The bond, it's so strong,
    As can tell in their eyes,
His fingers, in mane,
    As with gallop he flies.
It's over the fences,
    And back down the side,
And back to the stables,
    The two they will glide.
In comfort they lie,
    With gold straw all around.
And darkness now falls,
    And not one single sound.

Jacqueline Wilkins

An Angel

I send you this little angel
She comes from up above
She wants to surround you
With joy and lots of love

She feels you need some healing
So she's always very near
To protect and heal you
And take away your fear

This angel is always with you
Just ask and you will find
That you will feel better
Just knowing she's around.

Jean Ruddy

Beauty And The Beach

I stand at the sea and all that I see
Is the sea
But bored I am not
As this moment it is silvery
And shines like the moon in front of me
The last time I stood
In this place so deserted
With a violet pink in the sky
Stretched out before me
Was a velvet-like carpet, and wonder I do
Why this visa so striking
Is only appreciated by I
For the sea holds such beauty
Sometimes so peaceful and calm
But the tempest runs deep
With its current so fast
And lives have been taken and buried
So I stand here entranced
With the view ever changing
And my brain is devoid
Of my lifely commitments
I am at one with nature
And breathe with the waves
And it brings me a pleasure divine
For this wondrous sight
Soothes my nerves and my tension
And my wanderings along the shore
Can clear my mind
And bring back perspective
Of what in life there is to enjoy.

Susan Clough

Lonely Life

Through the long winter night,
I sit alone in the pale moonlight,
My thoughts are of yesteryear,
Upon my cheeks, brings a tear.

Dreams and love have gone before,
My heart will ache, for evermore,
Time is a healer, so they say,
How I wish you'll pass this way.

Life passed by, the years have gone,
I thought then, I need no one,
Now that old age is in sight,
Here I am alone, with my plight.

If only I could change the past,
Alas, my life is ebbing away fast,
Listen to my words, take heed,
Never think there's no one, you'll ever need.

Gladys Brunt

Remembering Betty

Betty Smith has very recently passed away,
Released from the cancer beast she suffered every day,
But she was brave, courageous and an inspiration to everyone,
Always with a smile and lots of fun,
Betty told it like it was, no beating around the bush,
You got it straight, never with a fuss,
No matter how she felt she would always help anyone else,
More often than not putting everyone before herself,
Her family and grandchildren gave her the strength to fight on,
There are no words to describe how they feel now she has gone,
God came to take Betty away from the cancer nightmare,
To be with Him in Heaven and comfort her there,
He wanted her to be one of his angels, that's why he took her away,
Now Betty is at peace and will never suffer another day.

Trudy Lapinskis

Mary Florence Alice

Can you hear my voice, friend?
Do you feel my hand clasping yours?
Tightly, because I do not want you to leave yet.
A life of ninety years or more is still not enough.
What will I do when you are gone?
Remember the frightening noise of the bombs falling?
Feeling the blast of shattering windows and plaster
Hitting us and miraculously finding we were still alive.
You working late into the blackest nights,
Guiding others through thick fogs.
Later when I was still at school we bombarded you
With snowballs, such a different time.
Soon I discovered romance, you had already found yours.
The holidays we spent, birthdays, Christmas, Easter
Celebrations of occasions always together.
Laughter filled our lives.
Now others take gentle care of you.
A stranger's blood courses through your veins.
Nourishment is through a clear plastic tube
And oxygen from a mask hiding your lovely smile.
Your bed ripples softly under your frail body.
I brush your beautiful hair, now snowy white.
Your husband and daughter sit full of sadness, weeping.
My tears come at unexpected times.

I wanted to phone you yesterday to tell you my hibiscus
Had one flower on already, yours is late this year!
Or early; maybe it waits for you in Heaven.
Now there is a stillness, no rise and fall from your breast.
You have already slipped away so quietly
To go to your eternal rest and leave me, in sorrow.

Christine Clark

Breaking Free

From out of the darkness
And back into the light.
I long to break free from
All the problems within my life.

Instead of being hidden away
Amongst nameless strangers' shadows,
Where I'm neither seen nor heard
By anyone right here and right now.

Then suddenly straight out of nothing,
I go ahead and start reliving a half-baked jaded memory,
With me remembering just how strong
From inside to out I used to be.

Now with this single thought I find
A single spark of courage deep inside of me,
Overtake all and any kind of doubt I once had.

So now I find myself getting back up off my knees,
And rising once more onto my feet.

But the very air I breathe
Lacks any kind of real energy at all you see.
So I scream out real loud and release
All the pain and frustration that's been building up in me.

Now I find myself breathing in sweet, clean air
As I now walk free once more,
From out of the darkness of others
And back into the light of the sunshine once more.

Peter Walker

Grieving In The Bedroom

I opened the wardrobe.
I thought I saw your lost shoes
hiding, abandoned,
their laces twisted,
tangled together
the way our two bodies
would tangle as we sank into sleep.

I thought that nightly melding
would hold our dread at bay
but the bed is empty now,
and when I inhabit it
alone
fears we stored there
come out and play on the pillow,
squatting in my ears and brain.
My legs splay without impediment
without comfort . . .

The duvet is all mine and I lie down
under its down,
stiff, still,
embalmed in tears,
my innards all plucked out.

Janice Windle

Untitled

The sea casts white horses across the Earth
The sands of time await new birth
Endless waves in an endless sea
Chasms so deep, canyons of mystery.
Dolphins so gentle, quietly knowing
Sharks so violent never slowing
Whales - gigantic elephants of the sea
Do these creatures hold the key
Of Man's existence since time began?
Do they know the Creator's plan?
Are they watchers, placed here to see
What Man will become; what we will be?
Will we erase war, hunger and greed?
Learn how to help each other in a time of need?
Not turn away from those in pain
But help them to live and love again?
To hold all in trust as caretakers of Earth
Or will there be a new rebirth?
Will we ever learn love is God's plan?
The Earth is His, it does not belong
To Man.

Elizabeth Allen

I Will Haunt You

I want you to remember me like this . . .
Each time you catch a wisp of auburn hair
Blowing in the wind
It will take you back to promenades
Of holding hands in borrowed lands
Every slender high-heeled limb
Echoes of mine they will bring
And when your senses guide you
To my smell . . .
Every last drop of my Chanel
Will intoxicate your mind
Each woman's curves that you admire
And everything your heart desires
Each small of back
Each curve of spine
Will be an exact blueprint of mine
Each lash-framed eye of deepest brown
All lip-glossed mouths will bring you down
Most slender necks will haunt you still
All swing of hips and spring of step
Each peach-skinned sheen
Or bend of breast
Every bit of soft-pink flesh
Will weave your senses and enmesh
I want that I will fan your flames
No future woman can take my name
If I can never have again
That love of ours which made me sin
Then forever in your mind am I
Breathe ghosts of me in every sigh . . .

Helen Hadley

On The Side Of Truth

'What is truth?' was Pilate's question.
Truth to you and me
are different things.
'You shall not kill - not even a fly -
why should they die?
This truth I feel.'
    'Are you a Jain?
    Do you believe that God is in all things
    that breathe and thrive?
    That's rich! I've never met the like before:
    all life is ours to take and utilise.'

'We've seen the truth!' the soldiers shouted,
'Truth to us and truth to you
are worlds apart.'
    'You shall not kill - no young nor old
    were born to die
    before their time.'
'Are you a pacifist?
Do you believe in love for all mankind?
A conscientious one?
That's tough! I've never met the like before:
your peaceful walk is out of step with mine.'

What *is* truth? A potent question.
Truth to him became the force
that cut her heart.
'I shall not lie - this pain is truth -
so merciless
I want to die . . .'
    'I'll make amends:
    you can't believe our love has had its day!
    It didn't mean a thing -
    that's true! I've never done the like before:
    can you and time forgive a fool like me?'

'What is truth?' asked Governor Pilate
of a certain Man.
'I am,' said He to all who seek. 'Truly.'

Linda Mary Price

Happiness

Is happiness a butterfly,
Elusive, beautiful to see,
Ephemeral and justly free,
Not to net, for it may die?

Is it self-forgetfulness,
In pursuit of greater aims,
Exuberance, joy, leisure, games,
Concern for others, gentleness?

Is it just for deserving poor,
Or those who empathise with such,
Not self-seeking or demanding much,
Rejoicing in love's simple lore?

Is it purity and peace,
Untyrannised by self or sin,
All harmony and peace within
As all desire and striving cease?

Happiness is in innocence,
But also in being forgiven.
Happiness is a glimpse on Earth
Of joy we may know in Heaven.

Happiness is a woodland walk,
And sunlight dappling the trees,
In companionship and talk,
Becalming once stormy seas.

Happiness may be a bluebird,
That comes to your garden to feed,
Or it may be a gentle word,
Or a thoughtful, kindly deed.

With luck there's joy in your labour,
It comes with making things grow,
In looking out for a neighbour,
In seeds of hope you may sow.

You find it in your dog's soft fur,
A horse's whinny and neigh,
In your cat's insistent purr,
In friends towards the end of life's day.

Happiness is a treasure
That is not won without cost,
Is impossible to measure,
And sometimes known only when lost.

There's happiness in creation,
Poetry, music, sculpture, art -
The spirit's communication,
Each heart reaching for the great Heart.

Happiness comes from letting go
Of lesser joys for a precious goal:
Perfect love; for then we may know
Reunion with one Divine Soul.

Jill Clark

A Child's Thoughts

I'm only a child so small and weak
Little to drink and nothing to eat
Where are you there to look after me
Will someone answer back to me?

I am missing my mum and missing my dad
This you will think so terribly sad
Please don't cry for me but stand up today
And help all the children understand and obey

I have something to drink and food in my tummy
And people give paper, pencils and money
God answered our prayer in life today
To help us to learn in our little way

I've now met up with someone I had lost
Who was risen one day and died on the cross
He is helping the people across the world over
So we thank you Lord a thousand times over.

I am only a child and now I've been found
And given a home, a small piece of ground
Thank you for finding time for me
I am off to my grandma's for a cup of tea.

Nigel Ball

The West Hatch Bell Tolled For Robert Bruford

I awoke very early on that misty morn,
And knew I would spy the brown-eared fawn.
He delicately caught the mourners' scent - where two hundred or more,
Had filed through the lychgate the day before,
When you, my dear uncle, were laid to rest.

From the edge of my bed in your little blue room,
Once my childhood retreat under the cobwebby coomb,
I watched over the graveyard and the sweet hallowed space,
Where the ancient tree sheltered your chosen place,
But the little brown deer walked on by.

I thought he would notice the fresh flowered mound,
But the dainty wee fawn gently picked his way round,
It seemed as if Nature had taken her own,
As the West Hatch Bell tolled on and on,
As the West Hatch Bell tolled on.

One thousand trees you planted for us, you cared for us all,
Amongst illustrious ancestors you stand so tall,
So, blow forever in the gentle breeze, rise with the sun and set in the west,
Keep weaving your magic from your place of rest -
Smile on our endeavours in your old special way.

K Susan Bradbury

A World Of Change

A black man, across the pond, speaking for change . . .
Normally it's passport-less white men who land this role.
This time it's revolutionary, incredible, celebratory.
A man who grew up in Indonesia! Who knows Africa's red earth.
Who has drunk with mad students and danced before a president.
Who lived on the poor side of town and read comics!
Read it for yourself. Shout all about it. The Earth has come together.
Yes we can.
Will it now divide?

Henrietta Cozens

Metaphorisms

Time back, country parts gave names to ways we act:
Power, the sun. Moon, mystery. Stars, arrays of hope.
Clouds, doubt. Mist, evasion. Rain, relief
For thirst in throats and the land's need to grow.

Ice gripped the Earth. Fire burned in air.
Wind blew sky-high, or crashed hopes down.
Trees thrust strength. Hills reached high aims.
Plains stretched plans. River and sea bore trade.

Apples spelt the fall. Nuts, the mad. Grapes, bitterness.
The rose, beauty. Lilies, the idle. Violets, shyness
Horses meant force. The bull, boldness.
Fox, stealth. Crows, theft. Trout, still calm.

All shut off now, beyond tight new windows,
In cars speeding past views, scarce glanced upon;
Or double-glazed in the house returned to, where no birdsong,
Or breeze pierces. Machines micro-whisk junk meals;

Or contact online chat; switch on tinny music;
Screen videos, of star drama, or soap trash. Who cares?
Answers once came from the grain of the Earth.
Now they lie in the media. Rawness keeps its metaphors.

Patrick Henry

Colin

I glimpse your eyes in the mirror
as they peer back at me from behind the faded curtain of my youth.
As I work, my body echoes your gestures.
My hands are yours as they close to grasp the stone.
When together our eyes show smiles at unspoken jest.
So here as your son I stand, so much of you within me.
But will I ever have your heart?
Trusting, giving and true.
My Father you are, my friend you have become, and so to stay.

Anthony Storey

The Road Is Just Ahead

Keep going,
Keep showing,
Keep moving,
Keep proving
You cannot see the light,
but it is alright
things are coming right
as in time you will see,
it is for the best
and the best is yet to be

Keep praying,
Keep saying
the dream will come through
a wonderful future is awaiting you

Keep working,
not shirking,
don't run away,
hold on for another day
the burden is yours just for today

So bear it
whatever the weight of the load
it won't break your back;
so don't look back,
you are on the right road.

Jo-an Carter

Deliverance

I'm walking very slowly to the dentist,
I'm feeling scared, and not a bit sublime,
I'm hoping that he'll say, 'It's too late to see you today,
Get another appointment for another time.'

I'm walking *very* slowly to the dentist,
His needles are quite blunt and two feet long,
And when there's a tooth to fill,
He gets this Black and Decker drill,
And makes enormous holes, while he hums a happy song!

(Later)
I'm walking very quickly *from* the dentist's
I've heard something that lightened up my day,
When I went in the surgery, gloomy faces did I see,
They said he'd a heart attack last night and passed away!

I said, *'Whee!'* and then, 'How dreadful,'
My face a mask of sombre gravity,
And now I skip away, reprieved till another day,
While he'll soon be filling his *very* last cavity!

Mrs Glenis Outhwaite

Freedom

F reedom is often far away
R etained in the hidden recesses of
E very trapped and tortured person's mind.
E ager to reach out and
D ispel all fears and entrapments
O f their day by day existence
M oving towards liberty, peace and harmony.

Ann McLeod

Community

Community means togetherness or folk living in the same locality.
It can, of course, mean an organised social body,
but . . . what does it mean to me?
Well, it means solidarity with people having a common cause.
All being united and acting together, these used to like
unwritten laws.

As a child I lived in a tenement where folk were friendly to everyone
All shared their dreams, trials and traumas and also shared
a lot of fun.
During the war and in times of trouble . . . being a neighbour meant
being a good friend.
Even delivering each other's babies and in times of death helped
out till the end.

No one dreamt of locking their doors and even the poor shared
their last crust.
Parents taught their own children to show respect and so we all
learned to trust.
Unfortunately, we're now living in a very different age and many people live in
fear.
So often children are out of control and gangs attack anyone near.

Schools are major communities but lack of sanctions make
indiscipline rife.
So frequently we read about pupils doing drugs or carrying a knife.
Churches are often half empty with tiny congregations and
many empty pews.
The Ten Commandments are relegated to history as just so much
old news.

The family unit is being corroded and this is the basic fabric
of our society.
I cannot even find in a current dictionary the exact meaning
of propriety.
We seem to be on a downward trend with no law or order as
we used to know.
Thus the lack of community spirit in some areas is the first thing
to go.

I feel sad at this decline in standards despite all the great efforts
being made.

To encourage and educate everyone to raise their game and reach
a certain grade.
If we all took responsibility for our actions and respected each other's
human rights.
Communities would thrive and become more alive with each person
achieving new heights.

Mary Anne Scott

A Matter Of Choice

No visitors called to the house
on the hill
but they did not care,
they had each other
and the little blue car
adorning the driveway.

Two or three times a week
it went chugging into town
its occupants stopping at the bank,
post office, chemist or supermarket store.
On the way home
a bottle of wine,
occasionally a bottle of Irish
for medicinal purposes.

Their garden was a paradise of flowers,
from hollyhocks, delphiniums, miniature roses.
The weeks passed by, season followed season
until one day one fell asleep
never to wake again.

There were no mourners.

Rosaleen Clarke

The Door

Three times I knocked upon the door
The answer came just as before
'We do not know the face you wear
We cannot breathe in your cold stare
Come back when you have found a name
That is not yours but looks the same'

Three times I tried to touch the sky
Each time I raised my arms too high
I had to look beyond the moon
My eyes had left my head too soon
Searching for a vacant place
All I found, an empty space

Three times I leapt into the pond
To see just what there was beyond
The water whispered as I sank
'You left your feet upon the bank'
Washed up on an unknown shore
So that I should jump no more

Three times I tried to chew my tongue
From which the stranger's words had sprung
I choked upon another's scream
That cried, 'You shall not have my dream
You must search to find your own
And learn to leave what's mine alone'

Three time I died but couldn't sleep
The hole they dug was much too deep
With nowhere left that I could go
My footsteps traced the path they know
I knocked upon the door once more
The answer came just as before.

Elisabeth Ware

Hope

On a cold winter's day,
With gale force winds
Howling away;
The raging sea causing tidal affray,
Sandy beaches in disarray.

On the apocalyptic horizon,
Dark clouds of derision;
In the blackened sky,
Thunder and lightning ride high.

In the distance - a boat,
Struggles to keep afloat;
On the shore - a lonely figure,
Paces without any trepidation,
Oblivious to all distraction;
Is it pure expectation?

Under my watchful gaze,
Soon he is a haze;
As darkness clears,
The lone figure reappears,
Holding hands with another;
Are they enamoured and paramour?

A distant clap of thunder,
And my mind no longer flounders;
Even a dreary day turns bespoke,
As I walk away full of hope.

Shamim Ruhi

A Mind-Polluting Piece

Within this room where all was still,
Where it all moved quite arrogantly,
I lay there having lost my feeling.
    The booze streamed down my throat
As though it were poured into a corpse;
Even that once dependable thing was lost to me.

As time is said to turn the mind straight.
I'd been in a dead-like slumber
For three weeks,
Hunger sated and my heart once more stepped on
Like a shopkeeper's face by cruel thieves.

I was still wretched and stuck
Within this cruel agitator, where my hobbies
Consisted of the dreamless.
    An oddly unfathomable time,
A perfect lacking of colour
                  And yet . . .

Jason Russell

God

I see you everywhere . . .
Seven days to make all . . .
But you continue to toil on, season by season . . .

Intricate crafting of the flowers . . .
The aerodynamics of the hornet fly . . .
The heady night flowers, hit the back of the head,
Stronger than wine . . .

Spiked green spears splitting to reveal the shiny brown conker . . .
The delicate, perfect features of the tiny mouse . . .
The sharp wind, fresh, blowing blankets of moody rain clouds . . .

The snow, pure, clean, beautiful beyond belief . . .
The old and new, running together . . .
I pray I never lose the wonder of watching your work . . .
I see You everywhere . . .

D Ritchie

Unhappy Memories

I lie awake, the long hard day is done,
I long for sleep but know it will not come.
The cold, dark room engulfs me in its grip,
The coughing starts, of medicine I take a sip.

I sit erect, the cough has had its way,
I know I will not sleep till break of day.
With eyes shut tight and hands clasped to my breast,
My earnest prayers are said for peaceful rest.

The morning breaks, I hear my father's tread,
He must arise to earn our daily bread.
My mouth forms words this hardworking man to bless,
But all I feel is worry and distress.

On ancient cycle he will wend his way,
Over virgin snow - where children soon will play.
On icy road a pickaxe and shovel wield,
But against the winter's wrath they are no shield.

My mother lies asleep on feather bed,
A night of joyous drinking she has led.
No call of duty will her slumber break,
No sacrifice of pleasure will she make.

I wash and dress in haste for school's sake,
There is no breakfast here of which I could partake,
Two icy gulps of milk from kitchen jug,
Not even time to find my old cracked mug.

And so to school - what will this day reveal?
That children sometimes can be very cruel.
But when the lunch bell rings at noon each day
That's when my popularity holds sway.

The children have had sandwiches and cake,
No room for dinner will their tummies make,
But I can eat the sum of three each day
If I eat theirs they will be allowed to play.

So hunger gone and feeling rather full
A sense of well-being fills my soul.
My fractured life will know a little peace,
The worries for a little while will cease.

Joyce Gifford

For Our Precious Young Souls

You are our future
We are relying on you
So see what you can do.
Hopefully learning from our mistakes,
Making it a better future for all the human race.
You are all special and unique,
Hoping the future be not so bleak.
All your energy needs channelling the right way
To make it all worthwhile one day.
So whatever you are doing, give it your best shot
You never know what will be your lot.
How great this world could be
To have no wars or poverty.
Our hope is in all you do
May God bless all of you.

Cynthia Fay

A Choice That Was Not Mine

A man may choose with whom he shares his life.
A woman has to be another's choice: to be a wife.
However much she longs her love to give,
That love may be rejected: as long as she may live.
For circumstances are the driving force.
'Tis they who will dictate a person's course.
Whether loyalty or duty rule the day:
Sometimes 'tis they alone, who have their say.
Then what is left? A well of love untouched;
A loving heart.
Dreams unfulfilled and shattered, far apart.
A loneliness and emptiness that changes not,
A sense of loss: a person time forgot.
How can you lose what is not yours to lose?
How can you miss what you have never had?
How can you grieve for one who has not died?
Only the heart itself can this decide.

Grace S Edgoose

Remembering Jon

Dear Mum

Remember that day six years ago
When I arrived at Jenkins Farm.
November the fifth I recall was the day,
Stables, huge fields and a barn.

It was to be a great start for both of us,
A wonderfully well matched pair.
Remember the days we would go for rides
In glorious sunshine, the wind in our hair.

Remember when I was a naughty lad,
Rug tearing was fabulous fun.
But then from somewhere out of my sight
I'd hear you scream, Jonathon.'

I would turn away and go into a sulk,
My nose almost touching the floor;
Then I'd gently nudge you on your hand
Until we were friends once more.

I've left a few broken toes behind,
A few dents in my stable door;
But the only thing I was trying to say
Was I love you a little bit more.

You gave me the best years of my life,
Stayed with me when things looked glum.
The story of my wonderful life began
The day you became my mum.

Time has gone so quickly by,
Much faster than we would wish;
But life's too short to pine away
So please mum, remember this:

When you're feeling sad and blue
Don't sit down and start to weep;
Remember that all these memories of me
Are yours forever to keep.
        Jon x

Carole Pickford

Water's Edge

Water's edge
Perfect day
Over a ledge
Now which way?
Hazy head
Swirling breeze
Blue overhead
Too much ease
Run through sand
Laugh at the tricks
Takes your hand
It's all too quick
On the edge . . .

Water's edge
Pouring rain
Different ledge
But here again
Views are the same
It's times that aren't
The perspectives change
You know I can't
Seeing in the dark
For the first time
Making its mark
I draw the line
At the edge . . .

Water's edge
Looks like always
In my head
It has betrayed
Pushed me too far
I didn't want to go
Sea appeared calm
Strong currents below
I never thought
It could pull me down
Yet I have fought
And I will not drown
At my water's edge . . .

Anna Robson

Gawn' Fur It

See thaim ower there?
Aye, thaim on the corner.
Look at thim jist,
a cavorting pustulance.
Petite batards, drinkin' bukie 'n' cider,
workin' thimsels intae a froth
fierce as Visigoths.

They're up fur it the night,
a'hm telling ye.
No fur them the sprayin' graffiti
ur liftin' car radios an' that.
Vandalism's mincin' ken
fur pussies an' weans an' 'at.

Public nuisance is naw fur them,
they're gawin' fur it big time,
brekin' an' enterin' ken,
an greevus boadily herm.
Bit only if they hiv tae, ken?
Pensioners is too weak tae fight back.

Hamish Lee

My Summer House

I love my summer house
It's so sweet
The only place I seem to keep neat
In my rocking chair I tend to doze
With Snowball my rabbit at my toes
It's where I watch nature at work
Far from the housework I can shirk.

Janet Chamberlain

Memories

It does not seem that long ago
Since the day when we were wed
The day you had to undergo
Changing your name to mine instead

Sometimes while sitting in my chair
I reminisce about days gone by
We truly made a handsome pair
As on you, I knew, I could rely.

The wedding ceremony was about to start
As you came walking down the aisle
I could not contain my beating heart
When I encountered your sweet smile

Now truly my life is so complete
Those special ways, and how you cared
My solemn wish is, may we repeat,
And cherish memories we both have shared

Throughout each day and in every way
I have grown to love you more
At night when I kneel I pray
Dear Lord, let me stay with you evermore.

David Blair

Bethlehem Babe

And I will lull you, my child, to sleep
Neath a ravished moon and a tempered sky.
And I will hold you in sweet embrace,
Tonight there is nothing you need fear nor dread.
For malignant midnight has clutched me
In her wanton arms
Leaving a spray of diamonds, with all her winged charms.
Close your weary eyes my yonder darling child
For the cold night is dark and the autumn wind is wild
Bethlehem babe, silence be your cradled sleep
Your holy hour is yet to come.
I know I shall still be here,
When the foghorn forlornly calls upon the dawn
Then shall I awaken and fly,
Somewhere dear to me
Where slumber sleeps
And restless heats shall yearn
Bleeping with the sunset
Yet sober as the dawn
With white wings softly started
Bidden towards their eternal flight.

Sean Conway

Untitled

They said just do it
Nothing to lose
So why am I lying here
So angry and confused?

When it happened, it happened
Just can't explain
The most amazing thing
Can cause so much pain?

You fought, we fought
Every minute till the end
I can't imagine ever
Having the strength for it again

Know you're still with us
And sometimes it's so hard
But you never need to worry
You made us who we are.

Lisa Patricia Macdonald

Where?

Where are the poets of long ago
Whose poems rolled off the tongue,
With whom I could thrill to a bugle call
And of battles fought and won?
Where are the poems that were written
in tears, that told of love, offered and spurned.
That I could recite with bitter delight,
For my heart with the same passion burned?
To hear once again a song of the trees,
Of meadows and old village spires.
And ardently listen to poems of praise,
That yesterday's masters inspired.
The poems I learnt when I was a child,
Still a chord in my memory touch.
For the heartfelt rhythm of the lines
Gave a feeling, one felt in the guts.

Jo MacKenzie

Dew Morning

Perhaps the dew isn't polluted
They say it's all under control
Below danger level so why feel uneasy?
There are smells entering the kitchen
But after a while gone
You've just got to get in and join 'em
Water's warm and 'luvly' once you're in
On a cold day it's warmer
Than when the sun shines
All a matter of contrast
And what you're used to

People still complain about cattle trucks
At rush hour peak period
But now we have smaller newspapers
To keep our elbows in

We accustomed ourselves to photos
Of kids with balloon bellies
Holding out their leaf hands

So let's all laugh nervously
We must enjoy a glimmer
Like dew on blades of grass
Sun shining this morning.

Pat Mear

Such Is Life

The ways of life move as on the waves of the sea
One day I am in the trough beneath normality
Then next I crest the wave on which I am exalted
And yesterday's problem is today's triviality

Why should this be, why is my life not one smooth path?
Where is the happy life that's trouble-free?
Picture a man whose way is paved with all his needs,
How can he know God's blessings if he never tastes adversity?

Bill Barnett

No One Sees

When I want to cry
No one sees
And if they do don't wonder why.
When I need to bleed
They wouldn't understand
Or see the need.
When I want to die
They wouldn't see the reasons why.
No one else needs to know
The reasons why
No one else needs to cry
Love you
Goodbye.

Simon Browning

The Baden Rooms

(In memory of Ken Smith 1955-1994)

Olive bowls and candlesticks
balance on the storm-broken oak
of your table;
crouched on a new floor,
of sycamore and elm.
Your hand-carved chair is empty.
All these echo Colebrook Close,
half of long ago.

Candle tongues whisper on the walls.
Their light releasing sap-scent
to colour the Baden rooms,
the frame and the glass
warming you,
frozen in the photograph.

Sian Hughes

3 Minutes

Saturday morning, blustery sun, I visit Dad in St Clare's.
His medication so strong now, of me is he aware?
I hold his hand, so thin and clawed
Not the protective paw of 'my daddy' anymore.
I talk *at* him gently, interrupted by the beats of machines
Eyelids flicker, a twitch of his arm, I hope they are blissful dreams.
I kiss his cheek, waxy now, skin so taut on bone
Stained yellow hue, visage so gaunt like the nicotine
Has come back to haunt this shell who gave it shelter.
I don't want to leave but Mam wants a CD from her caravan miles away.
To play her man a memory: Buddy Holly, 'True Love Ways'.
Start out OK, then get delayed, my brother has the key
So we detour, Mam and me . . . can't shake this sense of urgency.
On the open road eventually.
A call on her mobile: eyes lock and speak silently a while
No room for a word, nor a smile: I turn in the next quarter mile.
Purposeful, calm and safe, yet swift
This most important drive, this most important lift.
Straight for Dad's room, view of Primrose Valley.
Two nurses stop us, *'There is no time to dally!'*
Their faces paint a thousand sorrows
For Dad there'll be no more tomorrows.
'3 minutes late, Dad, I am so, so sorry.'
'Did you know, did you care?' Urge myself not to worry.
But this is my biggest regret, one I have not resolved yet.
Still, I just had to be there with you.
Every atom, pore screamed, *'You're still in the room!'*
I looked up to the corner of the ceiling, such a strong instinctive feeling
And I got to say goodbye, trusting my mind's eye
Which also pours with tears . . .

Vivienne C Wiggins

Speak!

I looked for the words
I looked in my mind
I looked to my conscience
And here's what I found

Words to be spoken
Words to be shared
Words to be cherished
Words to be feared
Words for the lonely
Words for the crowd
Words for the silent
Words for the loud
Words for the present
Words for the past
Words for the first
Words for the last
Words for the broken
Words for the cured
Words for the stained
Words for the pure

I spoke to my conscience
And it helped me to see
That words bring down walls
Between you and me
So let's speak!

Kevin Mahon

Observations

The bright blue sky is beautiful
With low clouds dazzling white,
So is the velvet darkness
Of a frosty winter night.
Studded with a thousand stars
Sparkling and bright,
A yellow crescent moon looks down
From quite a lofty height.
A shooting star streaks across the sky
In seconds it has gone,
Out of sight forever more
Where the universe rolls on.
There's the mysteries of the heavens
And mysteries of the Earth,
The mystery of our life itself
Our love and joy and birth.
And when our life is over
Our time on Earth is spent,
May our sins all be forgiven
And our souls rest in content.

Enid Hewitt

BOGOF

Trollies jostling in the aisles
People standing gassing
I seem to walk for miles and miles
I find it so harassing

With fruit and veg I'll make a start
Oh blast! This trolley squeaks
I throw some tatties in the cart
Must not forget the leeks

Onwards I go towards the meat
Chops or chicken or roast
Maybe tonight we'll have a treat
Or perhaps just beans on toast

I know I'll get some bacon
It's buy one get one free
So if I'm not mistaken
That's what we'll have for tea

Right now, let's see, where's my list
Bread, butter, jam, coffee
No there's nothing I have missed
Might just add a bar of toffee

The dreaded checkout comes in view
My trolley I manoeuvre
Can't leave now I'm in the queue
Forgot bags for the hoover

Never mind it's my turn now
But wait there's something wrong
My shopping they will not allow
The belt to pass along

I'm getting agitated now
The till is down this time
So now make myself a vow
Next week I'll shop on line.

Margaret Winkworth

Now – What Is Real? What Is Love?

Satan's evil is not physical attack:
He can only cast doubt on what is real;
Making some aware of what they think they lack
And where is confidence in what we feel?

Satan attacks by putting positives down,
Throwing sarcasm against all that's right;
'Antiheroism' has no moral crown –
Against such stuff how does anyone fight?

Amongst mockery, what is good any more?
Who knows *how* to stand for right against wrong?
As consciences are hardened *can* love restore?
Yet those feeble 'other gods' are *not* strong.

Too many religions are just being nice,
As they don't want to offend or cause wars;
Earning divine favour by avoiding vice -
Showing kindness towards some worthy cause!

Now Hubble's telescope views the Universe:
So how *Great* is Our God – Oh, can't you see?
Much more than a whim, a big bang or a burst . . .
What can I do to impress . . . **little** me?

Yet God gave His Son just to say *'I love you;*
Will you just listen to Him and believe?'
Overcoming death, miracles continue
To show us *The Father's Love* – just *receive!*

In no other name than Christ is salvation –
The Heavens declare worship in this age:
The Whirlpool Galaxy's God's invitation . . .
Starring *His Son on the Cross* - *that is Praise!*

Natalie Brocklehurst

Once Upon A Time

A tiny acorn fell to ground
Seeded itself and grew.
Tenderly at first,
Gaining strength anew.
Nurtured by the sun
And blue from the sky
Coloured by thoughts
As people passed under
Branches galore
Spreading asunder.
The acorn now a mighty oak
Known throughout the land
Exuding knowledge from its boughs
To feed the happy band
Of folk expressing themselves.
With words and rhyme
Hopes, thoughts, dreams
Love and gentle calm
From pens that do no harm.
Now the day has come
It's celebration time for you
You've come of age
Oh! Mighty one
Those you gladly helped along
Now join in praise and song
Voices raised
This day we bless.
Happy Birthday, 'Forward Press.'

Marnie Connley

'Dropwing' A Special Friend

The remainder of those feathers
Lying on the grass
Will forever be a memory 'of days
Which now have passed.
For that chubby little blackbird
Whose wings were out of line
Seemed forever present' in the garden
-all the time.

His birdsong from the willow tree
Was wonderful, indeed,
And his ever presence near me
Was rewarded with a treat.
For this very special blackbird
Had a beauty Heaven-blessed
And in spite of his deformity
He stood out from the rest.

With colourful robin, greenfinch and thrush,
None could compare with this bird
Who stood out amongst them in so many ways
Though comparisons may seem absurd.
He was so tame and trusting,
Which sadly sealed his fate,
But the indelible loss I shall always feel
Can never be replaced.

Joan Mathers

A Funny Thing

What is love? So many say,
Does it even exist?
True love seems so elusive
They wonder if they have been missed.

Love seems such a funny thing,
Trust, respect and stuff,
We make it all so complicated,
Then it's not enough.

They say there are all sorts of love
But that's a misconception,
Which leads to much unhappiness,
Why buy into that deception?

This pure and true emotion
So little understood,
Has no rhyme or reason,
Although we wish it would.

However, if we could accept
That love just is – that's all,
Then love's not such a funny thing;
Love's just love, is all.

Bridget Holding

Rescue In June

'Look, Dad!' my youngest little son
Tugged at my sleeve in his urgency,
In the back garden pointing, 'Look, look there!'
Where the yew tree sat in its green despair,
Grown all leaning from fighting sea breezes;
In depths of its sombre leeward side
The wretched captive fluttered and shrieked,
A fledgling sparrow, this year's child.

The pale beige cotton thread had perhaps
Been stretched to guard some new-sown bed
Or escaped a wind-taut washing line;
Now bound her ankle, the claws a-twine
And as she'd landed on barren branch
Had snagged all about it and hung her there.
My hand's quick swoop strait-jacketed her
Open beak panting, her small storm stilled.

And so I held her, whilst my son fetched
Small sharp scissors, spectacles found
In my pocket. At a careful angle
I snipped away at the Gordian tangle
Brushed away severed loops of thread,
Freed her at last, and let her go,
Cheeping, on freed legs hopping away
Under the bushes and out of sight.

My son called out in half an hour:
'Its mother's feeding it on next door's lawn.'
And so I felt a moment's peace, some kind
Of thank you from the embattled world: release . . .

R G Head

Fly With Me

Excel
At trying
To flying
Impel,

Observed
A heron
Not airborne
Unnerved,

Appoint
Drive skyward
Paths plywood
Enjoined,

Assume
No helper
But willpower
Abloom,

Attempt
A take-off
From back-off
Exempt,

Commence
The lift-off
No switch-off
Prevents,

Above
For heading
Wings spreading
Enough,

Unbound
A wingspan
No linden
Around,

Prepared
A flightpath
A triumph
Declared,

Ascent
Not scuppered
By upward
Intent,

Aloft
In azure
Hues hazier
'Be off!' ed,

Across
A mountain
No downturn
Because.

Robert Murray-Graydon

This New Sky

So it's true,
And they said,
So we walked to the river instead,
And the sky,
So we saw,
Rose and rained; we watched fall,
Then it shone,
Saw the sun,
As it gilded our hearts for the run,
So it's right
And I smiled,
Or tried as I could for a while,
Any breath,
Every hand,
That it touched turned back into sand,
Yes we knew,
Then we left,
Leaving footprints and seabeds bereft,
This new sky,
And our sea,
Washed my heart back to you,
Straight from me.

Rowena D R Carlton

Minefield

A picture of
A minefield is there
To be studied
As it hangs
From a bare wall
To scare and startle
To induce despair
Through shock,
Skill of brush depicts
Havoc, horror
Calamity and
Nature's wounds
All in sepia.
A woodland copse
Its trees torn, branches
Bruised and brutalised
Now naked and exposed.
Twisted roots uplifted,
Grasses crushed
Flattened by forces
Exploding from
The shattered earth,
Mounds from which
Bury all that still
Can live. Echoes resound
There's a loudness that
Deafens and horror
To seal the eye.
A smell of death
From such aftermath
Then - stillness, quiet,
A minefield slumbers
At rest. The picture
To be studied, remembered,
Questions still
To be asked.

Elizabeth A Hackman

The Seat

It's just a simple wooden seat
But sit awhile and view
The river and its estuary
Its waters greenish blue
The warm and golden Cornish sands
At Padstow and at Rock
To where the famous poet lies
Asleep at Enedoc.
This seat is dedicated to
'A gentle Cornish man'
No famous poet was he,
And yet in his life's span
He won the hearts of many
With his kind and gentle ways.
He is no longer with us
But the memories will stay.
I only wished he'd realised
How much respect he'd earned
As he was self effacing and
He never would have yearned -
For fame, for that was not his way
He lived a quiet life
He dearly loved his family,
And most of all - his wife.
He did not know how many came
To make their sad farewells
Sincerely sad and sorrowful
For he was loved so well.
And now there's just the simple seat
In a spot he loved to view
Where a man who shared so much in life
Is sharing it with you.

Dianne Shorthouse

Images Of Max

(For Mum And Dad)

Black, glossy, smooth, domed head,
Spread out like a jellyfish on the tiled floor,
Eyes matching the tiles –
Warm glowing colours of a winter fire,
Eyes that remind you of the melancholy of autumn.
What spirit he has!

I put my arms around him,
Solid, whole, self-contained dog!

A delicate, sensitive, shiny black nose
Sniffs gently with intense concentration
At a spot on the ground,
It seems to have a life of its own!

Sitting out, black as the night, smelling the moon,
Off on a midnight jaunt.

Years pass.

Walks, staggering, drunkenly over uneven ground,
Yet retains his dignity. His spirit remains.

Huge, open heart, continual exchange and share of love.

Victoria Hazard

A Sea View

From the grey roof of the hotel building, the birds stare at the sea,
They are four herring gulls, and for them the view is free,
Perched higher than the best rooms, and soaking the sun's rays,
With no need to open curtains, for such a perfect gaze,
A grand array of colourful boats, shine from the harbour below,
Packed in tightly at the quay, they have nowhere to go,
The sparkling water beckons them, to glide across the blue,
Dazzling like white diamonds, to lure any boat and crew,
The herring gulls continue their watch, above the guests below,
Who reside in darkened rooms, away from the sun's glow,
The birds revel in their freedom, staying where they please,
In contrast to the hotel guests, ruled by locks and keys,
Intrigued by the fishing boats, some people stop and stare,
At the many nets and boxes, designed to catch and snare,
Do the birds feel hungry, when they see so many fish?
Destined for our dinner tables, or an exotic dish,
The gulls remain on the roof, and watch the world pass by,
Enjoying the sun like everyone else,they have no urge to fly,
From thier perfect vantage point, the birds stare at the sea,
They are the rooftop residents, and for them the view is free . . .

Stephen Norris

Lost And Found

The days fly past and you're not here
No smile from you to fill the empty air
The darkness falls
But there's no love wrapped in it,
Cold and moonless
Lonely, dark and bare.
But in my dreams I see you just returning
With open arms
And smiles to light the sky.
My wandering soul was lost along its journey,
Now sees with just one touch,
Through Heaven's eye.
How thin the veil, between this tired world
And all the mysteries within our minds.
That we can touch, without a hand
And find our peace
When in reality we're blind.

Giselle Harold

Losing Dreams

Who drew the line between sky and shore?
That line that lifts the eye to soar with others wings
To see the freedom, giving grace to leap the heart to wish,
To open wide with hope to live a dream of endless chances
Beyond the line, spread on a canvas of what could be.
The blameless blue will outline what we have
And the more familiar shore deceives.
For the shifting sand won't hold that you were there, however deep.
Relentless, washes through footprints left when you are gone,
Leaving only echoes of laughter drifting in the tide.
So if not now, then dreams will disappear,
Lost to only memories and might have been.

Wendy Richardson

Freedom

I once went to a circus
Where I saw a huge brown bear.
Around his neck he had a chain,
And danced for the people there.

I saw the sadness in his eyes,
And knew he did not care,
To be inside that circus ring,
Where people did not share,

His sorrow and confusion,
His anguish and his pain.
He only wanted freedom,
From whence he once had came.

To be out in the forest,
As free as he should be,
And not performing in a ring,
For the likes of you and me.

I never do go back,
When a circus comes to town,
For I think of that poor tortured bear,
Who dared not make a sound.

With tears in my eyes,
I watched him as he danced.
And with great sadness in my heart,
Knew he had no chance.

Of ever gaining freedom,
So oft' of which he dreamed,
Never more again to roam,
Beneath the sun's warm beams.

Carole Bloor

Thy Spirit Failed To Slumber (First Love)

'Twas to me alone that wayward brood
Thy heart grew quick and fonder,
Was it half a dream while in pensive mood
That thy spirit failed to slumber?

For was it fair to say that love was true
In all its form and splendour
To have loved me then as I loved you
So warm, so young and tender?

And was it on a day where clouds lay gay
Or were they grey and sombre
And were those fields full of loving pain
Or only my wish to wonder?

And was thy kiss not the one of bliss
That your heart should rove and wander
Or are thine lips the one's you miss
While thy spirit fails to slumber?

Abby Winter

Becoming

The joy of becoming who I was always meant to be
So swiftly broken or so it seemed
An unending moment as one heartbeat stopped
And the other faltered
A glimpse of Hell on Earth
Juxtaposed with her sweet and radiant face
Yet as she grasped my hand with her waning strength
I saw the newborn arise for deep despair
The horror shall forever be nightmared in context
And through a growing veil of tears
I felt her in my arms,
Bienvenue au monde, nous esperons que vous passez un
bon sejours,

She opened up a single eye
And turned to me and smiled.

Simon P Rossiter

Someone To Turn To

Where should you go when you want advice?
It's so confusing and not very nice.
When you've got a problem you want help with,
And so many people have an opinion to give.
But no one has your interest at heart;
They don't care if your life's pulled apart.
'They'll be your friend and will help you through,'
But they're never around when you want them to!
They say that they understand,
But just don't want to hold your hand.
They appear to be on your side –
When conflict comes they just hide.
They agree with everything you say,
Until it comes to backing you some day.
But don't despair there is a friend,
Who'll be with you right to the end.
A friend that's closer than a brother;
Unconditional like no other.
One that's there in every fight,
On call day or night!
He'll always tell you what is true
For He really does care for you.
So make a friendship that will last,
And on Him your cares can cast.
He'll share in your pain,
Again and again,
He'll even carry you through!
For He *always* knows just what to do
And He loves *you!*

'Our help is in the name of the Lord, who made Heaven and Earth'.
Psalm 124:8

Melanie Biddle

Morning Flight, London – Kent

Dawn, just before sunrise,
The smell of damp grass
A bumpy take-off
And the elderly biplane –
A DH Tiger Moth – lifts gently
Up into the misty air.

We climb slowly into the calm
June summer air and watch the fading
Lights of London's night begin
To disappear. Suburbs and city
Slide past below until we find
The grey river thread and start
To follow it eastward.

Then suddenly the rising sun breaks
Through the mist and the Thames
Shines out mercurial silver, serpentine,
Stretching out into an ever widening estuary
Heading towards the English Channel
And the North Sea.

The engine drones on, the slipstream
Thrums and sings through the wires
That brace our aged wings – we bank,
Circle out and in pilgrimage pass
Over Canterbury on what seems
As blessed as angels' wings.

Richard Storey

Winter

Sitting by a fire transfixed in a gaze,
Logs crackle splintering,
Startles a room full of talking,
Shadows forming.

Through a window frost turns
The grass white
Day has become night.
A hedgehog finds its way
To a safe haven.

Tomorrow we will go walking,
Wrapped up warm,
Amble beside the sea,
Picking shells.

Dogs on leads, excited,
Some having races
Happy faces,
Sniffing, finding driftwood.

Boats tethered by withered rope,
Water lapping at the bow,
In the fading sunshine.

Waves climbing high on to rocks,
Gulls squalling.
Fishermen hauling their nets,
Hoping for a good catch
Before storms come calling.
Snow starts falling.

Brenda Russell

Country Walks

I like to walk in the countryside at any time of year
And see how the changing seasons create a different atmosphere.
Like running to take shelter from sudden springtime rain
And listening to the whistle of a distant passing train.
To walk across a meadow past fields of new mown hay,
Hear the rumble of a tractor as it goes upon its way.
Inhale the smells of the hedgerows when the weather is gentle and fine,
Watch the changing shapes of fluffy white clouds,
Like sheets on a washing line.
To look across a valley and down into a dell
And see a wisp of woodsmoke and the sound of a little church bell.
I've crossed over fields and styles and gates
Watched villages busy with summer fetes.
To see the corrugated look of fields being ploughed,
Hear the seagulls and rooks screaming out loud.
Listen to the buzz of insects, of birds and cows and sheep,
Lie down under an oak tree and gently fall asleep.
And now the autumn approaches and the weather starts turning cold,
The leaves have started falling all bronze and copper and gold.
They're ankle deep upon the ground.
I love walking through them just to hear the sound.
I have very often wondered though
Where do all the leaves suddenly go?
We're reaching the time of year now when farmers find to their cost
The fields are hard as iron and covered white with frost.
The sky is grey and leaden, the trees are bare and stark,
It's only mid afternoon, but already getting dark,
Each season has it's own beauty
And i really love them all.
From ethereal early morning mists
To a land covered with white snowfall
It's nearly turned full circle, soon it will be spring
The flowers and trees are coming to life
And the birds are starting to sing.

Michael Harrison

As Handsome Did

You always talked such rot about
your hair, trying to pass its slight
performance off as an event,
buffing your baldness up with
monagrammed bristle brushes
and defying me to find any grey.

Sometimes you even clamoured
it was growing back, rejuvenated,
so you said, and I'd have to
marvel at your unnatural cleverness.

Sometimes the way you corkscrewed
as you slept would set a wispy
bit of down the wrong way round,
and then you would lament you'd been
too prodigal and grown too much.

And every time the barber finish off
your timid back and sides,you spouted
endless desperate tosh all through
the rest of your pink-lobed aftrenoon.

But what about the trim for vanity!
in the full eye of your shaving light
you'd slowly tilt your chin about -
moustache, nose, eyebrows, ears, all
synchronised with classical precision.

'What a dashing fellow!' you'd explain
when you were done. And Mum,
of course, would say you were
as handsome as the Prince of Wales.

For years i've kept your brushes
pressed together, hedge-hogged, safe,
inside my dressing-table drawer.
but still your stardom dodges past
the breathing bristles; and your
silver monogram still shows off.

Erica Warburton

The Old Man

I looked at the old man sat in the chair,
I wondered how long he'd actually been there.
I saw such sadness in his eyes,
Before he stared at me, in surprise.
Suddenly his eyes took on a look of hate;
His hands started trembling at quite a rate.
He seemed to think I was someone he knew,
As he slowly got up to join the queue!
But then he remembered the queue wasn't there
And once again, slowly sat back in his chair.
He muttered something about a plane,
The guns being fired, again and again.
How he wished he had died that night,
Gone through the tunnel t'wards the wondrous light.
It was then that I saw a tear on the cheek
Of this lonely old man all withered and weak.
It was then that I realised his heart was still raw
From the blood, pain and tears created by war.

Christine Glover

Telegraph Poles

Climbing the hill from the village
We'd hear the eerie music high above
Telephone wires looped from pole to pole
Humming a mysterious song

I used to think
That the birds sitting on the wires
Were writing the notes for the music

I would stretch my arms around each fat pole
Putting my face to the warm wood
And feel the thrumming
Of the messages whizzing past each other

Between people up above and far away
Who didn't know I was there.

Merle Tshiamalenge

Closer Together

My nerves are tingling as we lie on the bed
The feel of your thigh against my leg
The heat spreads through my body
We're moving closer together

I reach out, brush your soft tender lips
Your tongue warm and moist caresses my fingertip
I touch your hair, running it through my hands
It feels cool as silk, the flames are fanned

You move on top, pinning me down
Your breath on my neck sends shudders down my spine
You stroke my face, nuzzling in close
Nipping my ear, I've let you nearer than most

Our eyes meet like a smouldering fire
The air crackles, the tension gets higher
Time stands still, we can't look away
Forever like this I want to stay

In my mind the kiss was a must
But it's a 'whump' in my face and I'm told not to lust
The fight resumes, the pillows fly
To my precious moment I say goodbye

As you jump off the bed pulls me to my feet
And, while the music still plays its low tempo beat,
You move me into your arms and we start to say.
We'll move closer together another day!

Helene Garvie

The Weekend Match

Tired and exhausted
Tom needed a break
So the first one offered
He decided to take

He said to his wife
'Our team's playing away
Do you mind if I plan
An overnight stay?

Friend George has offered
I can stay there the night
With him and his family
Will that be alright?'

Wife Mary agreed
To him going away
As long as he returned
The following day

With high hopes of winning
Tom felt ten foot tall
Till his team for some reason
Kept losing the ball

With egos deflated
Cos they didn't win
The two drowned their sorrows
At the local Swan Inn.

When the landlord called time
They could no longer stay
So as drunk as two clowns
They staggered away

Early next morning
A bright sunny day
Tom still a bit tight
Was snoring away

When George came to call him
Saying 'Show a leg mate,
I've in store a surprise
So we mustn't be late.'

As Tom with great effort
Got out of the bed
With legs still wobbly
Nearly fell on his head

While he showered and shaved
And drank two cups of tea
Tom wondered to himself
What the surprise could be

Now George being the driver
Of course knew the route
The surprise he mentioned
Was a fair and car-boot

Tom had never been to
A car-boot in his life
Though had often been asked
To go with his wife

When Tom and his friend
Arrived at the boot
Tom was standing amazed
At the sight of such loot

There were plates, pots and pans
And soft toys for kids
Furniture and bric-a-brac
All open to bids

Now Tom spoilt for choice
Seeing this 'n' that
Saw down 'neath the table
A backless black cat

He turned the cat over
As it lay on the grass
It was shiny and new
With a collar of brass

The lady on the stall
Agreed it was nice
As Tom rather shyly
Enquired the price

She said 'It's a bargain!
Is this pussy door-stop
To you it's a pound
Would cost ten in the shop'

Soon as Tom saw the cat
He had Mary in mind
And was chuffed to have found
This unusual find

In the meantime his wife
Not having to cook
Was off to a boot fair
For a leisurely look

As Mary was leaving
A man shouting his wares
Said 'Lady I've a cat
With green eyes that stares

I have also a dog
A black cow and some sheep
If you want a bargain
Come over and peep'

She peeped in the basket
And boxes with care
Then found the black cat
With green eyes that stare

But strange as it seems
'Twas all front and no back
But she thought, *what's the odds*
It's cute, shiny and black

While looking it over
The man said 'It's a cop
A wonderful pound's worth
Is this green-eyed door stop.'

With the crowds dispersing
She walked home from the fair
Whilst cuddling her cat
Enjoyed the fresh air

With the men's boot over
The two stopped for a snack
Tom collected his car
And made his way back

While Tom made the most
Of a beautiful day
The time it seemed endless
Since he'd been away
When Tom arrived home
And got out of the car
He was very surprised
To see front door ajar

Clutching his present
He walked in through the door
Only to be met
By a black cat on the floor

He thought to himself
This cannot be true
That I have a present
That adds up to two

He couldn't believe it
That there on the mat
Was a beautiful green eyed
Grinning black cat

Bitterly disappointed
Not sure what to do
He couldn't tell Mary
'I've a present for you'

When she already had one
All shiny and black
But he did have the notion
It could go out the back

Some hours later
Coming in through the back door
Mary was surprised
To see her cat on the floor

She shouted to Tom,
'Have you moved my black cat?
Something has happened
I'm not sure what!'

But Tom didn't answer
He'd gone out the front door
Leaving her moggy
Still there on the floor

She totally puzzled
Went to answer front door
And nearly fell over
Her cat on the floor
Now positively shaking
Thought, *this can't be true*
When I thought I had one
I'm the owner of two

In the past Tom and Mary
Had longed for a cat
A beautiful moggy
To curl up on the mat

But Mary was allergic
To animal hair
So cats were a passion
The pair could not share

Till fate intervened
In a strange, quirky way
A remarkable outcome
To Tom's overnight stay

When Tom returned later
He saw there by the door
Two grinning moggies
Placed on the floor

And his wife also waiting
For his answer to say
What had he been up to
Since he'd been away

Tom then explained how
He had gone to a fair
And saw amongst clutter
A cat lying there

He spoke to the lady
And asked her advice
She thought it a bargain
And so very nice

All through the summer
The cats sat on the floor
Each doing their duty
With their back to the door

Come the chilled winds of autumn
Creeping under the door
The cats lost their position
There on the floor
With coats black and shiny
Each one back to back
The pair now resembled
A Siamese black cat

Now close together
Both sitting as one
A cat on the hearthrug
An object of fun

With the onset of summer
No longer a pair
You will find them once more
Letting in the fresh air

Two green-eyed moggies
On front and back door
I'm sure Tom and Mary
Will not want anymore.

Marvis Lyn-Dahl

Mother Nay

The angry orb is yet to scream
To fetch the dark away,
To finish off the blackest night,
To breach new light of day.

The swollen hills of clouds in slumber
Await the birth of rain,
To drench and douse
The veins of leaves,
To soak parched lips of pain.

Of pain they cry! Such supple sins
That pass beyond her face.
A face of pure, unbridled hope,
A face once blessed with grace.

'Awake! Awake!' the flighted caw,
'Awake dear Mother please!
We yearn to flock and flurry fast,
To sail your gentle breeze.'

The prickled mice awake in awe
In hope of Mother's touch,
In lust for warmth and newborn sun,
To feel her love as such.

'Such love!' they cry,
Her woodland pines,
'Our mater will not wake!'
For Mother Nay,
Has left today,
Her burden she can't shake.

A world once bronzed with natural grace
Has lost its fight as one,
Dear Mother Nay
Gives up today
Her kingdom, sadly . . . gone.

Lauren Sheridan

World War One

Sometimes I simply sit and ponder,
While gazing out on our garden green;
Had I lived at the time I wonder,
What would my fate in the war have been?

A call-up letter through letterbox
Would change my destiny, with each word;
Perhaps with a baby in the pram
And family left so ill-prepared!

Would I have joined in the revelry
With friends so willing to do or die?
Then seeing them show such bravery
But witness too, many brave men cry!

Could I have survived the stinking mud
With shattered bodies scattered around?
Putrefying in a sea of blood
And me pinned down on the spattered ground!

Should I have mingled my fear with rage
At human folly of wasting life?
Bad memories left not to assuage
And feel contempt for the futile strife!

Yet evil forces when they conspire
To threaten our cherished freedoms' way,
Leave little choice but to raise such ire
And defiant, risk the deadly fray.

Many with valour did freedom serve,
Who died or endured – I know not how!
But lasting gratitude they deserve
For I can ponder in freedom now.

Bill Newham

Aboard The 7:38

The Transpennine Express
And. Its Metro-strewn coaches, emptied coffee
Cups. Clutter.
        The chitter
Chatter of youth, and the cries
Of the newborn punctuating the stillness

Snaking through the Meanders of tracks,
Circumventing the Pennines
And the extensive expanse of unending landscapes.
Its phallic loveliness, redolent perhaps of you
Trails in our wake.
Its beauty undimmed
        In the palimpsest of trees
Doubles as a stoic reminder of you . . .

Skin new as its landscapes in spring
With eyes transparent as its tranquillity.
Heady with desire, your fair hair
Coursing your outlines,
Marrying your skin like its heather-thronged plains.

Your glow fades in the distance;
But
Inside this capsule
Your lover awaits.

Ejike Ndaji

Lincoln

The Cathedral
Is a giant on the hill.
It calls me home.
In its splendour and loftiness
There is room for me
A modern day pilgrim
To make my requests
Give thanks and sing
All to my God who dwells within.

Who for centuries has made this
His tabernacle, His resting place,
And pilgrims have come
Through history, as I do now
And sat in the nave in the cold
Straining to hear the word of God
Whilst gazing upwards and all around
At the enormity, the majesty
Light and shade of the stone, medieval glass.
God moves among us caressing us
Holding us up
As the music and choir begin

Would that I could stay for always
In this, my spiritual home.

Kath Taylor

Good Old Days

You've heard of pastoral
The ideal story of life in the country:
The romance and glory of doe-eyed calves;
Of gambling lambs' tails; of maids in bonnets
With yokes and pails.
'Rubbish! Poppycock!' you robustly say.
I say, 'Come and help us load the hay.'

The sweet seed grass is brutally laid.
Green corduroy landscape tedded and brayed
As belching tractor, swathing its way
Whilst the dust-dry molehills away.
We don't see woodmouse and slowworm die.
Patient crows watch 'til their chance comes by.

Finally, that regular clatter,
The trammel and thump of compressed matter
As bales are dropped like stones in a pool.
The driver, Bob, must unhitch and refuel
Before the huge trailer comes into view.
The rest is a matter for me and you.

Bales too heavy to lift with ease,
Trussed with red twine's hand-blistering squeeze.
'Shan't wear shorts if I do this again!'
'Lend me some gloves to ease the pain!'
Scratching stems and prickling thistles,
Red eyes and noses and asthmatic whistles;
And all that noise and all this heat
Far too hot to want to eat,
But oh! so thirsty, tired and sore,
'I can't go on . . . oh no! There's more!'
Never so dirty, never so tired;
Never bath time and bed so greatly desired.

Now diesel smells and noises are done,
Silence descends with the sinking sun.
Prim Bellis Perennis closes her eyes to sensual night and
all it implies.

But for those who choose to linger there,
Constable's 'Haywain' just cannot compare.
The cockle of roosting pheasant at dusk
Shattered air heady with elderflower musk.

Crepuscular nightjar mowing his lawn
Masks twig-crack and call of a hungry fawn;
Rufous cubs start to play as they did
When their wily ways Sweet Vernal hid;
And bats in fur-and-leather gear,
Gnat-wise, bare-toothed, fly far too near.
We, too, go hunting in case we miss the final romance,
The lovers tryst.
The female glow worm's lovesick burn,
Her desperate ploy lest 'he' should spurn.
'Light of my life,' she seems to say,
'Come to me on this longest day,
Under the moon and the dogrose bowers,
Come to me for these few brief hours.'
Honeysuckled hawk moth quenches his thirst.
Will nightingale's shivering passion burst
From the black thorn hedge silvered by moonlight?
Might he deign transcend a perfect night?

Denise McCann

My Mum

We all had one
Not everyone has one
I have mine
Time goes by
You forget to say
'I love you'
It's never too late
It's almost too late
Just call her or write
Someone to weep at
Someone to shout at
Someone to smile at
Someone to count on
My Mum.

Olivia Gribble

Is Democracy Democratic?

A democratic government have we:
Rule of and by and for our citizens,
Yet oft, the most of us will disagree.
Decisions made that seem to make no sense,
But made by those elected by us folk
Upon a manifesto we agreed,
And voted them our leaders, not our yoke!
To never disregard us, but to heed
The voice and will of the majority,
Who placed them into office, gave them power,
We, through our taxes pay their salary,
On us their jobs depend, when come the hour!
Democracy can thrive so long as they
Remember to serve *us*, not go *their* way.

Christopher Head

The Answerphone Message

I'm not here right now but on a different plane,
Hiding amongst the pages of a good book,
It may be some time until I'm out again.

In this word-built world I've found, good wins the day,
I cannot hear neighbours rowing through thin walls,
And I have no cares or urgent bills to pay.

I nestle safe between the covers, on the run,
Enveloped in new adventure, untroubled
By the knowledge that the housework is not done.

If you wish, wait for the tone, then have your say,
By I won't pick up the phone as I'm not here,
No, not in mind and spirit; I'm far away.

Jennifer Wardley

Victim Discovered

Show me, know me,
tell someone about me.
Take no temperature, no pulse, yet if you think
I am an angel I think that
I might still grieve from far, in the
distance we cannot share.

Above, below,
you will think of shadows.
That I have knelt at night
before the dawn laid me down.
The darkness of another place;
unconscious, with the cold to hold
my hand; till carried home.

Be gentlemen,
for I was gentle too.
Uncover me yet
cover me in your care,
in your dignity stay with me.
Then take not leave me lying there.
To a better place I know.

P Butler

A Darker Shade

When the night has been painted without stars
And hope has become a darker shade of sun,
Rustle now some words unto the silent moon,
For life is a ghost with apple green eyes
That walks this Earth homeless.

I claw the sky with helpless hands,
An August cloud over sands that whisper 'no name'.
In Darfur, time has so many anguished faces,
And life . . . leaves no shadow upon the ground.

Norman Royal

The Scotland I Love

Hills and mountains climbing into the clouds
Snow covered peaks all year round
Gushing streams down mountainside in waterfalls
Quiet canals with boats drifting by and heading for scenic lochs
Their passengers sunbathing on decks of blue
Navigating canals lying in their path
Low-flying clouds giving mysterious and eerie hilltops
Gigantic hydros to give electricity to the people
Fish ladders for the migrating salmon leaping upriver on their way to spawn
Huge, lonely moorlands where battles have been fought
Where the wild birds dwell until the shooting season begins
Blue skies, sunshine, rain or snow
Never ending lochs their beauty to see
Investigating the myths the locals relate
Hamlets to visit miles from civilisation
Narrow roads to manipulate while climbing high
Castles to visit and admire with fabulous gardens abound
Seas to cross by ferry carrying the post, food or equipment
Silent nights, enormous starry skies with no street lighting
Shadows falling from high above onto the lochs creating imagery
                                            of more depth
Mirror reflections from tree lined land
Forests of trees, a variety of firs, covering hillsides
This is the Scotland I love.

Margaret Monaghan

Fading Away

Dreams and hope and knowledge
For a world inspired by peace
We know the Earth survives
By the mystery on lease
But lies, deceit and power
Are steeped within their souls
And all the efforts taken
They never reach their goals
They make their war on paper
And sign the darker deals
And send the young to die again
On crimson poppy fields

Do we have a hope at all?
We hear the old ones cry
Do we have a future?
The adolescents sigh
Care has fallen through the net
And infants melt away
Lies, deceit and hatred
Are the order of the day
Death becomes the Earthly feast
Where all the nations feed
Those blind and blinkered leaders
Swollen with their greed

So decisions must be made now
And truth must set the rule
And he who cannot manage this
Wears the headpiece of a fool.

Pamela Aldred

Too Late

'Too late' two words encapsulate
The saddest words in any tongue.
We know that fate has seized control
And there's no more than can be done
It was perhaps within our grasp
To change the course of what might be
But then the moments swiftly pass
Our good intentions, history.

Maybe some things are preordained
Set in an ancient destiny
Our heart feels nothing can be changed
Knows well that what will be will be
Yet hope lives on in spite of all
Till it is lost beyond recall.
Regret remains to haunt our years
A legacy of hidden tears.

Frank Flower

Faith

Where do we find our strength
When all seems to have gone.
When hopes have doubted
We have to keep going on.

Yet down beneath from our soul
A strength of spirit comes
To look ahead with a fountain
Of bubbling life to help us all along.

Our faith strives us ahead
From unforgotten thoughts
We've had our hopes there
All the time, I must keep gong on.

Audrey Porter

Dark Night

In the dark, ghostly, moonless night
Wind groans and moans with a sigh
There's an eerie chill in its flight

From a wood an owl hoots out of sight
With a warning to prey nearby
In the dark, ghostly, moonless night

Powerful wings glide using their might
With a swoop a battle is nigh
There's an eerie chill in its flight

The hunter intent on survival fight
Employs its nocturnal eye
In the dark, ghostly, moonless night

A rustle - a movement ever so slight
Then a shrill and terrified cry
There's an eerie chill in its flight

Helpless the victim surrendered his plight
Like the wind he was doomed to die
In the dark, ghostly, moonless night
There's an eerie chill in its flight

Margaret Smithyman

Doors

For every door that closes, another opens wide.
For every dream that comes to naught, and every tear cried.
For every opportunity we miss along the way,
Another chance presents itself, a chance to save the day.
If we could only grasp each chance and enter each open door,
Our lives would be fulfilled, complete, we'd never want for more.
Yet, often the door we do not see, it is hidden in the gloom,
We are trapped by disappointment, our lives become our tomb.
Cast off these binding shackles, break from your stifling past,
Grab every opportunity as if it were your last.
For some day in the future, your last chance it will be,
To grab the opportunity, to set your spirit free.

Charles Harvey

The Sea

Friend or foe
In times of calm so peaceful is she
Tranquillity of a high degree
Transport of delight.
Drifting . . . dreaming on a
Never ending solace . . . the sea.
Slowly, in ever changing mood or temper
Arises the wrath of nature
Crashing, thrashing, devastating waves.
Throws caution to the winds of change
Rises to a towering height
With a hand of destruction and might
Be still, be calm
But be afraid . . . or not
Of this, friend or foe.

Helen Tait

Pain Is A Strange Companion

Pain is a strange companion
She sits heavy in your heart
Saturation overwhelms you
As you look for a place to start
Afresh maybe or just run away
From sadness that swells like a sea
Reflected in a mirrors question
Of when did that become me?
And as the midnight moon rises
Lost tears begin to descend
From a whisper in the darkness
If this heart will ever mend
So hidden in this space and time
Of things that have to be
Pain is a strange companion
Only she can set you free.

Josie Dexter

Be Who You Are!

I saw a magpie on my windowsill
He'd come to take my troubles away!
He said, 'Go now be free again,
Go and be who you are,
Be who you are!
Life's just a feeling be what you are,
Go and do what you do,
Go and be who you are,
Be who you are!
Go with the flow don't worry so,
Be who you are and you will know.
Go with the flow be who you are
Don't worry so and you will know!'

Vincent Rees

The Signal

A signal from a distant star
Said Man is not alone,
From somewhere light-years afar
Aliens were on the phone
But scientists disagreed,
Some said, 'Just what we need,
Their knowledge - let's talk around the clock,'
But others warned of culture shock
And that the callers could be hostile,
After a while
It came to a fight,
Computers took fright
The signal was lost
And Man, still storm-tossed,
But alone again.

M Sherlock

The Peaceful Place

As I sit here in the stillness
Such a peace envelopes me,
Praise and worship rises upwards
To my God, who holds the key.

As I gaze at winter sunshine,
Soaking up it's warming rays,
So my heart expands within me,
And is filled with love and praise.

As I watch the Guernsey lilies,
Nodding heads in gentle breeze,
So my soul is filled with wonder,
And I'm taken to my knees.

Thank you Lord for so much beauty,
Everywhere, for all to see,
How I bless You for my garden;
This beautiful I long to be!

Patricia Ann Hendy-Davies

Pause For Thought

Life passes us by so quickly
It's gone with the blink of an eye
We're left only with thoughts of what might have been
And questions which always start, 'Why?'

When a child, life can seem endless
One day can go on and on
But as we grow older, time's precious
A lifetime doesn't even seem long

All of a sudden we're ageing
With so many things left to do
Why didn't we get them done sooner?
For our health is now fading too

There are so many places to visit
Ambitions still left to achieve
To think we'll get started tomorrow
Is so foolish a thing to believe

So if there's something you've always wanted
A dream that you'd like to come to true
Try as hard as you can while you're able
The only one who can do it – is you!

Jane Ricketts

Last Night It Snowed

An uncanny quiet fills the air
There is silence everywhere
No laughter from the girls and boys
Even the traffic's not making a noise
Last night it snowed!

There's no one walking down the street
Where are the people I usually meet?
The gates are closed, there's no school today,
That gives the children time to play.
Last night it snowed!

The traffic now has come to a halt
The government says 'Well it's not our fault
The grit and the salt are all running low
But in any case, it's the wrong kind of snow!'
Last night it snowed!

Now snowmen appear in all sorts of places
With carrots and stones to make up their faces
It's great to be young out playing all day
While the older folk wish it would all go away.

Last night it snowed!

Jean Dean

This Is The Morning Of My Life

This is the morning of my life,
Be still and watch a star-drenched sky
Herald dawn with soaring music,
As drifts of swallows soar and fly.

Stretching forth I reach the sunshine -
Source of life and warmth and growth,
New power again and rising glory,
Golden rays that seek the truth.

Daylight rushes forth from darkness,
Life force powers the world anew.
I am here to greet this moment,
And my breath drinks deep the hue.

Bless me Father this new morning,
Take my hand but let me stay,
Be my guide and comfort ever
As I step into the day.

Kristin MacEwan

Five Days

(Written whilst living 2 miles away during the Buncefield Fire December 2005 on a sleepless night at 2am)

Day 1
Thick black acrid smoke,
A burning funeral pyre of pollution.
As the plume chokes the sky, so it can't breathe,
The fluffy clouds are cumulus nimbus
This fire and brimstone is hell on earth for
Our town, our community, our planet, our world.

Day 2
As I lie awake in the black, and cough,
Thoughts rush upwards billowing
Tumbling out to choke me.
An acrid taste fills my mind
My thoughts turn grey then black
Thunderclouds fill my head
Why can't I extinguish them?

Day 3
What will the world be like?
What will or town, our community, our family, our world
When the flames of fear are extinguished?
Who can rebuild the demolished?
What will happen to our planet, our water, our air, our Earth?

Day 4
Still I can taste the smoke
In my mind, my mouth, my breath.
Windows shut, doors shut.
I can't get out - history has been written.
Inside there is uncertainty, fear.
Outside hope awaits in my world, my life, my job, my future.

Day 5
The sun rises in a dusky pink sky.
Clouds are cirrus - soft and white and warm
The grey smoke lurks still
No longer acrid, but wispy,
Like floating cobwebs, spun across the clouds.
Time to open windows, open doors, move forward
Into my world, my life, my time and breathe freely.

Katriona Goode

A Fear Worse Than Death

I have a terrifying fear
That's with me all the time
I don't get any respite
It completely rules my life

I am arachnophobic
And I cannot say the word
I used to call them *der* spi's
But now they're just bad things

I have to scour the rooms I enter
Dark corners fill me with dread
I have to check all ceilings
So they won't land on my head

I can't stand their little homesteads
They give me the creeps
As they mean that one is round about
And could get me in my sleep

I hate the green things on tomatoes
As they are so alike
So when I see one on the floor
It gives me such a fright

They creep and crawl throughout my life
On my towels and in my shoes
In the mirrors on my car
And through my head at night

I can't go in the garden
As there's more of them outside
I suspect moving bits of fluff
I've really had enough

You're meant to love God's creatures
And most of them I do
But *damn* that bloody *der* spi
It really has to die.

Cathy Weeks

From Your Daughter

As I gaze into my daughter's eyes,
As you once looked into mine,
I'm awash with fierce devotion,
All devouring, yet sublime.

You held each bruise and cleaned each graze
And kissed away the pain,
You've understood each tear I've shed,
Helped me to find my feet again.

You cradled us through deepest grief,
Pulled us back up to a level plane,
Chased away the darkest clouds,
Whilst both parents you became.

You're the only witness to my first breath,
Through to these words here now shown.
You guided me through right and wrong
From a child to this woman grown.

For all you've given and still openly give
Keep guiding our feet to safe tread.
Thank you is not enough to say
And I love you not often enough said.

So as I gaze into my daughter's eyes,
So innocent, untouched and naïve.
I hope to be as good a mum to her
As you have been and are to me.

K M King

The Quest

Ever travelling, not arriving,
no end to the futile race -
always restless, ever striving,
hoping to discern my place.

Summoned by the sea to travel,
called by mountains to the height,
promising they might unravel
purpose in my headlong flight.

Ever seeking, never finding
meaning in the journey's end -
never settling, always winding
round another hopeful bend.

Is the journey its own reason,
defying chaos to defend
disorder through the sorry season,
meaningless at winter's end?

Is the purpose just surviving?
Is the fate to ever roam
through a life of desperate striving,
never finding my way home?

Michael Gray

Folkestone Harbour

Gazing over the harbour wall
What has happened to it all
Where is all our fishing fleet?
Sold off no doubt, with debts to meet.
The harbour once was thriving
Fishermen adequately providing,
Their families all well fed
Contented and happy it must be said.
Father, son, cousin and brother
All looked out for one another.
The boats went out with the tide
To fish the Channel, long and wide.
Sea of blue and so deep,
Fishermen working while we're asleep,
Pulling in the lines and trawl
Hoping for a massive haul
Haddock, plaice, soles and cod
If there are many, thank you God,
The weather they depended on
They couldn't fish if the wind was strong.

Even when they weren't at sea
Their time was not at all free,
The trawlers needed painting
The lines required baiting.
With nets spread along the ground,
Holidaymakers were spellbound,
At skill needed for them to mend
The time that they had to spend
Weaving the needle up and through
A fascinating sight to view.
Crabs and whelks being cooked,
On the stalls how tasty they looked,
The old tan copper, I recall,
We kept warm against the wall,
The whelks to be picked out,
We hated that without a doubt.
All the sights, sounds and smell
The fish, cockles, the salt as well
The beach, the sand, the ebbing tide
All made up the seaside.

The fishermen were men apart
Fergie, Bob Kittens and Alfie Hart.
The Wallers, Taylors and the Heaths,
Spearpoints, Brickells and Featherbees.
Just to name a few
Characters that I once knew.
The Bakers, the Sharps and Darkie Fogg
Remembering them all has made me sad.
They all lived in one street
And made up our fishing fleet.
The community so close knit
On rough days along the harbour they'd sit.
They worked hard and played together
Why can't things last forever?
Now they have all passed on
The fishing fleet has nearly gone,
Just the odd boat here and there
The harbour looking very bare,
It's really not the same at all
Gazing over the harbour wall.

Barbara Andrews

Reminiscence

I remember, you must too, when every day wore a lilac hue,
And every balmy summer night, the stars outside cast diamond light.

The hedgerows greener, the heavens blue, the bursting buds of
Primrose bloom, flying ants and fluffy bees, maple trees with crimson leaves.

Days spent swimming in slimy ponds, outside playing 'til daylight gone
Windy days on pebbled beaches, rocky caves no sunshine reaches.

Sticky fingers, eating sweets, tiring walks in fields of wheat,
Birthday teas that Mum had made, musical chairs and cherryade.

My reminiscence may, I think, be coloured a biased petal pink,
But retrospect should always be, full of fun and wild inaccuracy.

Julie Dixon

Untitled

The golden veil of summer that shines love's glow upon winter's
                                                darkened heart,
That stirs within, to tantalise, it separates the reasoned mind apart
To raise hopes high, to cast them down,
In love's tight threads forever bound,
So fear is such, we trust in love,
Though we can crumble it to dust,
To bathe our dreams in love's slipstream,
A foolish care, so it would seem,
Though nature allows humanity, we create love's quality
So echoes of love's wilderness can breathe eternally.

Claire Woolmore

Muse

He is sleeping now, somewhere over my right shoulder,
But he is different to the beast that stands with me
Against the white-trimmed and capped features
Of the darkened street.

He is different, from the tall yet shrinking man that
Looks me in the eye and questions me to the soul and asks:
'Where do you go? Show me that place from which you draw
The will to stand, and I will show you where it ends.'

And I will reply, 'It is sleeping now, somewhere in the corner.
It is lazier than I and finds no peace when that which surrounds it
Slips from view and is replaced, so seamlessly as to go unnoticed.
Because to him each drop of the wave is bound alone and chatters as it flows.
This is why he seeks to lie between the contours of intention and of doubt.

I do not know if he will return to work today,
But I will hammer on and rouse him if I can.'

Jamie Carmichael

Puppy Love

Was it true love that we tasted
Or just our puppy love
When I kissed you for the first time
With the taste of bubblegum
When we pledged our hearts for always
In the sunshine of that day
With our bodies close together
On young love's tender way.

That day trip to the country
That walk along the woods
And stopped there for a cuddle
A squirrel paused to look
Our thoughts were held together
You said that you were mine
We missed the train just once again
For we never had the time.

With the first sweet taste of passion
Your sister stopped to call
We hid inside the bathroom
There's no one home at all
When danger passed we both sat back
And laughed until we cried
She must have known that we were home
We'd left our bikes outside.

Sweet moments of those summer songs
Life's loving youth that lingers on
Those eyes of blue I loved to see
That funny coach ride you and me
When people said, 'Those silly two'
But only there were me and you
Those songs we sang were out of tune
My funny girl, my Valentine.

Robert Walters

Dinky

There was a dog called Dinky,
His coat long, black and slinky,
Out he ran onto the road!
By came a lorry with a heavy load.
'Come back, come back' the owner cried,
But Dinky ran on and there he died,
The owner lifted him, eyes filled with tears,
His Dinky's dead after all these years.
I warned you, Dinky every day,
That on the road you cannot play.
The owner's heart thumped on his breast,
As poor Dinky he put to rest.
Five little girls loved Dinky too,
This brush with death the first they knew.
Their mum came home from work that day,
'Oh Mum,' they cried, 'Dinky's gone away.'
Their mother choked at their dismay,
Brought them close and began to say,
'Come now girls listen to me,
Dinky's not dead, he's alive and free,
He lives in a world just a thought away,
And when you sleep he comes to play.'
They lifted their heads and smiled with glee,
So glad in the knowledge that Dinky was free.

Marina Vaughan

Shoes, Shoes, Shoes

Shoes, shoes, shoes,
As we know are meant to
Be worn on feet.

But to own a brand new shoe
Is like breathing in fresh air
On Arctic circle,

To have a new pair of shoes
Is to celebrate a new birth,
To buy new shoes feels
Like owning an emerald and diamond
Brooch,

To shop for a new pair of shoes
Is to feel liberated,
To a woman buying a new pair
Of shoes is like
Being on top of
The world!

Famed for their magnificent designs,
Styles and colours, shoes will always
Be adored by women the
World over.

Joana Efua Sam-Avor

Reaching

Once upon a lonely hill,
A little girl sat cold and still.
It really hadn't been that long,
She couldn't think what had gone wrong.

Surely they can't be so bad,
To make her feel so very sad.
Why can't they see her hurt and fear,
These people that she loves so dear?

Where are they now she needs them here,
To share her grief and wipe her tear.
Would it really be a trial
To sit upon the hill awhile?

Inside the fire is warm and bright
And keeps away the deadly night.
While relatives all gather round,
She sits and wonders why she' s bound.

The girl they love, they hold and hug,
But she can't see them through the fog.
She laughs and talks, but on that hill
The little girl sits cold and still.

Bronia Rudzki

Lingering High

Sun stretches out on evening sky,
Ocean reflecting glowing light.
Up above clouds lingering high.

Far in the distance, mountains lie,
Almost hidden, well out of sight.
Suns stretches out on evening sky.

Water rolls in on sand so dry,
Tide mark rises, ever so slight.
Up above clouds lingering high.

Overhead birds eagerly fly,
Circling together, gaining height.
Sun stretches out on evening sky.

Footprints erased, memories die.
Sun slowly fades, makes way for night.
Up above clouds lingering high.

Day disappears, time travels by.
Hazy glow is no longer bright.
Sun stretched out on evening sky,
Up above clouds lingering high.

Katie Smith

Chip Buddies

Two rather little fat chips, decided to go along to the gym,
They thought if they did some working out, they just might get quite slim.

They did some kicks and punches, and jumped about a bit,
Then they were feeling rather worn out, in their attempt at getting fit.

They tried and tried without success, the inches did not go,
At least that is if they did, it really did not show.

They put in so much effort, it really was a shame,
They tried so hard to lose some weight, but it stayed on just the same.

They carried on regardless, with an optimistic air,
They rather quite enjoyed it, so they really did not care.

Then one day there came along, much to their surprise,
Two rather tanned and lovely, slender curvy fries.

They got on well together, and things were rather good,
The chips showed off their various skills, well they did the best they could.

The fries thought they were rather nice, they thought them fun and bubbly
They didn't think them too fat at all, just rather cute and cuddly.

After all is said and done, it really doesn't matter,
If you are really rather slim, or just a little bit fatter.

Maureen Woolard

The Whale

Breaking the watery vaults a black land emerges
Leviathan is born spouting like a Jonah, a vomiting womb lets forth
An erupting Vesuvius of seas batters the wooded ark
Call me Ishmael for I have seen arched over me a Kraken
Of dismal gloom.

Alan Porter

Slippage

Old friends
Asleep by the fire
battered and torn
worn out by desire
no finer resting place
for their weary soles
a couple
mates
content in their roles
left foot
right foot
not that it shows
together their
similarity grows

until one day
they'll be deemed unfit
too large and floppy
a bad habit
a dangerous pair
at loose on the stair
cast aside in a bin

their one deadly sin
too comfy by far
a terrible scar
on the landscape
of an orderly life

Sonia Singer

Valour

Just cause, not always fair fight,
We link arms in our plight.
Be it army, navy or marines,
All as one in times like these.

Status, money and pride too,
Above all the honour in you.
Sat chatting around the fire,
In uniform never to retire.

The laughter ceases, orders are in,
Drop lunch, we're going in.
Shallow breathing, sweaty palms,
What keeps you going: 'We'll come to no harm.'

Happy thoughts, *It'll never be me*
But there's always someone, wait and see.
Upon return, memory hazy,
Exhausted, wounded, physically lazy.

Negativity omitted,
Conversation limited.
And on minds friends and family,
But not for long – stay focused, happy.

And so sat down again, some but not all,
Those left, waiting for the next call.
A solemn sight, emotions hollow,
We give our day for your tomorrow.

Andrew Barklam

Carbon God

God of carbon, stardust
earth and trees
of Eden's waking rocks
of diamonds, clays;
in carbohydrate trails
mole molecules
God of proteins, peas
who lights our eyes.

God of Earth we've damaged
torn, polluted;
hydrocarbons, oils
in smoking skies;
through Jet Stream, wind and flood
marauding desert,
God, we cry to You
through rising seas.

God of life and truth
of cities, peoples
where, trading fears and hopes,
the lone word dies,
till love's resolve alone
restores, rebuilds us
as God weaves age and youth,
makes smallness wise.

Michael Brueck

Where I Was Born

(For my Husband)

The house still stands
Where I was born.
The gas-lit front bedroom,
Where my first breath was drawn.

Up to the new front door, the same old steps.
Once constantly rubbed white with donkey stone.
Traded from the old man, with pony drawn cart,
Who shouted 'Rag, bone!'

The sloping wall,
Provided me with a slide
And permanent holes in the trousers,
From the bumpy, rough ride.

The dusty back alley, through a gate,
Where many a battle was fought,
A bike shared and marbles,
Won, lost, swapped and bought.

On Mondays, the smell of washing,
Wafting upstairs and down.
Dripping clothes, dolly tub, rubbing board,
A steamy kitchen but never a frown!

An old tin bath,
In the yard, an outside loo,
Now it has a bathroom with shower
And central heating, too!

We didn't have much money
And not much to eat or wear
But as long as I had my family and my cats,
What did I care?

Mum worked hard and saved up to have
Electricity put in and a television, for me,
So I wouldn't need to go to the neighbours,
To watch theirs, from their settee!

It saw all the hardship and all of the highs.
It saw the family grow.
The happy family gatherings and most of all,
The love, that overshadowed all the low!

The bedroom that saw life come,
Saw my dear Grandma go.
The front living room window there,
Where she lay at peace below.

After all the upset,
Mum didn't want to stay,
A new life beckoned, so mum, boy and cats,
All left that house and moved away.

Now, in later years, every time that I pass by,
No matter who or what has come or gone,
In my mind's eye they are all still there,
With the little boy, that life still carrying on.

Sheila Valerie Baldwin

Our Land So Precious

Golden light on waters still
Throws shaft fragmented mist unstirred
Hangs muted, shielding dew-drenched webs
Of wonderment o'er fragile earth,
Strikes Willow, Birch then
Silent Swallows, regimented circled
Flight, caressed by brilliance casting
Shadows radiating early morn, from
Whence a stranger to these shores trawls
Tirelessly midst waxy wings, meets
Mother Nature, costume ruffled,
Enter ghostly reticence; Spellbound,
Tantalising scene along the
Hedgerows cramped and narrow
Fields of parchment
Scorched and arid
Sterile armour framed by Mallow.
Arching torsos bathed in Jasmine, sunshine,
Warmth with auras seeping, scenic glow
Horizons scanned, parade
A passion, blue sky show.

Geraldine Sanders

Mother Earth

My love is an island,
She wears a wrap of azure and Prussian blue,
To a backdrop of volcanic eyes
Which spill filtered light in golden tinges,
Blowing it back in sense and sensual shimmering.
For she is the radiant mother,
The sanctuary pearl.
Her body is God's study
Her mind locked around lay lines,
Arched and forever distant to the horizon's curve,
She will be the cherished dust
That settles the nerve for a tired mind
Who wandered in love with her deep.

David Williams

The Unseen Enemy

Time to face the enemy.
Are you listening?
I know it's not your intention to take prisoners.
You seek the ultimate victory.
Death is always your aim.
What will gainsay you?
Medicine? Therapy? Willpower?
I scoff at your invasion.
You think you have the upper hand,
But I give you fair warning that I will not go down without a fight.
So let battle commence.

Elaine Setohy

So Don't Conform . . .

The dead eyes of the dead son,
Stare dead towards the dead world.
Where dead fish on a dead sea,
Float dead towards the dead sand.
And the dead men walk the dead shore,
Eating the dead flesh of the dead ones.

So don't conform . . .

The dead roads of the dead land,
Lead to the dead ends of the dead towns.
Where the dead minds of the dead ones,
Happily play dead in the dead slums.
And the dead minds with their dead heads,
Walk the dead streets with the dead.

So don't conform . . .

The dead sky weeps dead rain,
On the dead flowers and the dead days.
Where the dead walk in the dead light,
Praying to the dead in the dead night.
And the dead heads with their dead minds,
Worship the dead Truth dead.

So don't conform . . .

Albert Pollard

He Wore A Pointed Hat

In outsized pants and pointed hat,
He knocked upon the door
Of a little old lady dressed in rags,
The poorest of the poor.

'Just a wee minute,' rang her voice
From down the threadbare hall,
As her dowdy slippers shuffled along
On well worn heels, so small.

'What can I do for you today?'
She asked the caller there
'I've come from a far away land,' he said
'Have you some tea to spare?'

'Come in, come in, I have some tea,
And you are welcome friend.
But alas there is nothing left to eat
Soon I must meet my end.'

'Oh dear,' said he, rubbing his nose.
'Oh no! I can't have that.'
And he wriggled his long bony finger,
Nodding his pointed hat.

And to this day nobody knows
How she came to grow fat,
But at another poor old lady's door,
There nods a pointed hat.

Sharon Marie Johnston

Epping Night Forest

The calm branched trees
Stretching out over forest floor
Reaching into midnight hour,
Where badgers peruse.
Powerful foxes gallop paths
Making way to back-garden dinner.
Ponds ooze life
Wind rustling bulrushes.
Darkness descending.
Moon makes face
Shines into every crevice.
Insects claw their magic
Bark cracks.
Rabbits dive among the mounds
Golf course provides.
Horses clop across impassioned roads
Leading coastally.
Couples court
Carefully caressing;
And new life arises for another day.

Melanie Littlebury

Early Morning Street Song

Dawn breaks slowly on forgotten men;
Unshaven, grey skinned, drawn, they greet the sun
With snarls and angry curses as they wake,
Spitting in the dust of better days
That dances spirals round their shuffling feet
Trying to hold them to Earth's time-blown body,
Trying to absorb their blood,
Their dust.

Condemned to watch each bitter new day form
They do not see some poet's holy flower
Unfolding sun-kissed petals in the heavens;
Beauty cannot exist within the range
Of hollow eyes that rake the sky unseeing
Then fall into the bottle that is clenched
In trembling hands as they search for an answer
In that liquid's bite to ease their pains
And change the clashing colours back to patterns
Even their torn minds can comprehend.

Their dreams are spoiled,
Grotesque, soiled, corroded,
So ugly now they cannot be believed
Impotent words and memories contort truth
As life stagnates, stilled pools, in day's great heat;
Just one more drink might start those waters flowing,
Just one more drink may hold the past at bay!

Dawn breaks slowly on forgotten men.

David Peden

For Another

I usher in the month with anticipation
This could be a shock of the new
My levelling the land
My defining time

Is it that we rely on another to define us?
If I sit alone is it valuable time?
Is ignorance acceptable as my reason?
I fear not, as we learn what we have as it leaves

Maybe concentration can lead to persuasion
Is it a crime for one to follow their heart?
As one follows their heart perhaps another heart breaks
You can't change what is done

As I retread Groundhog Day
I feel different
Do I care less? Have I merely found equilibrium?
Am I resigned?

Perhaps none of these, perhaps some of these
Maybe I have a different path to walk
Some things we love but we can't have
Mine is perhaps meant for another.

Jonathan Curry

A Cold Spring

The house is still and warm,
We feel safe inside these walls,
Outside the wind roars round like some primeval dragon,
That blows and howls thro' every gap,
And oozes under doorways.
Awake, we listen to the sound of rain-dashed window panes.
The darkening storm, and icy squalls
Seem far beyond where we still lie in comfort.
We hug the warmth and try to sleep,
Before the morning rising calls.
And so the spring arrives, no warmth or azure skies,
Just rain and biting winds.
The flowers droop and slowly cringe
Into a mire of sodden blooms
But it will change and soon the air will sweeten,
Warmer winds will hurry in to herald spring.

J Stenton

Helping Hands

Think a little of others
When you're feeling down
Your sisters or your brothers
Or someone in a crowd.

A helping hand costs nothing
So lend one now and again,
A little help is soothing
Kind words can ease a pain.

While you are helping others
You're not thinking of yourself
You'll forget all that bothers
And your heartache wouldn't be felt.

They may not stop to thank you
And struggle to raise a smile,
Remember how you felt too
Forgotten now, for a while.

Janet Emery

En Route to Emmaus

That road that day!
Sand-blasted, pebble-dashed
Under a brassy sky – yuk.

We trudged along, getting away,
Away from the damned city
(Where women wept, not knowing why)
And we grieved not just for our friend
But for our dreams, dashed into the dust,
Our hopes blasted on Golgotha.

Heart-sore we trudged on
Exchanging a word here, pain-pregnant,
Another word there, hopeless.

Then this fellow appeared astern,
Dust scuffing up from his heels,
Casually unknowing of the city's turmoil -
Strewth! Had he been on another planet?
We asked ourselves.
So we filled him in on things.

Now the words came tumbling out
Cascades of horror at the bloody end -
The memories were unstoppable, insupportable,
'Oh, my God, oh, oh . . .'
We too, like the women, wept.

In silence we trudged on
Until the stranger's voice slipped gently
Into our train of thought;
The train of pain was boarded
By passengers - love, sacrifice, hope, redemption, salvation.

There was spring in our steps,
Hope in our hearts as we footed it to Emmaus
There he blessed and broke our bread for us - that was it!
Our man had come - and is with us still.

Brian Blancharde

Shaving With Blunt Razors

one dare not ask
nor choose
this chaotic pattern

shapes that come in day and night
frost through sunshine
that hold
captivate

my destroying attempts to decipher
viewed through a distant haze
of destroying attempts

the source can never be found
yet still bleeds
stories of a time before man
from daunting woken nights
and innocent sleepless eyes

a gentle face
scarred by tired hands

Darren Powles

Chocolate On Horsey Beach

A sun raw tongue,
Solder charged
And spittle ripped,
Drips lactating flotsam,
Raft like,
Down green seamed hissing rock.

The frill foamed coffee head,
Percolates a frown,
And in whining anticipation
Of canine plunder,
Makes off,
Across a fast sliding shore.

Steve Harman

The Year

Winter passes
As winter always
Must
And spring
Steps in
On flowered feet

Whimsical spring
Merges
Seamlessly
With slow, heavy, burning
Dreaming summer
Who only waks
To welcome
Autumn.

Brisk, vivid leaves
Crisp underfoot
While
Overhead
Clamourous, gale-riding geese
Fleet south
Dragging winter's
White skies
Behind them.

White sky
White world
Ice stills the stream
While hedgehogs dream
Of slugs
Cold is cruel
To birds whose beaks
Seek frozen worms in frozen ruts
But

Winter passes.

Gill Atkin

What's In A Number

What's in a number!
A listening ear
Non-judgmental
To what . . . they hear.

So many troubled souls
Packed together . . . like blackened coal
Make their mark . . . left and right
Are these souls . . . from others . . . out of sight

Rows they stand in . . . ones and twos
Taken to the brink of death
If only . . . they could leave the queue
In their minds . . . there's nothing left

To nurse their pain . . . both in and out
Always there . . . day or night
Someone . . . to talk to . . . or even shout
Never! . . . will the light go out.

What's in a number?

Sylvia Connor

Journey Home

With the frost still icing the topmost branches,
The beeches are ghostlike
A grey mist against the black bronze of the yews.
The low sun, full on the slopes, is softening the shadows,
Bringing the trees to life.
Surrounded by silence I sit here, looking at the striped beige fields
Bordering the wood.

Enveloped in a cloud of joyful distraction I turn the corner.
Shockingly, the hill blocks out the light.
Winding ahead the road is dark, lined with ivy-infested trees.
On the sodden verge lies the body of a badger. Overcome by sudden desolation
I struggle to hold onto
My former delight.

Another corner and another
Then once more I see sun on the trees, peach now and
Purple - an affirmation!
Gratefully I turn my head and again face the light.

Jennifer Willmott

The Gateway To The West

'The Gateway to the West' it's called - this is Bristol's other name -
A city steeped in history
Since before the Romans came.
It is set in natural beauty
With the Downs so vast and green,
And there are many other places
Which enhance its beauteous scene -
Like the woodlands at Blaise Castle,
Ashton Court and Leigh Woods too,
And the gardens, with the animals,
All on view at Bristol Zoo.

There are many Churches in the city
Which our hearts and minds inspire -
With the towers of the Cathedral
And fair Redcliffe's mighty spire.
- The Suspension Bridge at Clifton
Is a wonder to behold
Showing Brunel's great technology
Which brought benefits untold.

The old iron ship 'Great Britain'
Is safely berthed back here once more
She was salvaged as a rusty hulk
Beached on a Falkland's shore.
The great feat of restoration
Makes a fascinating story,
At Great Western Dock she can be seen
In all her former glory.

This great historic city
Is long famous for its trade
Of tobacco, sugar, chocolate -
And finest sherry here was made!
The Avon, flowing through the Gorge
Between the ageless rocks,
Has brought ships of every shape and size
Into the City docks.
Here many, many years ago
This river's tidal waves
Shipped in very different merchandise
With cargoes of poor slaves.

The ravage of the wartime years
Saw Bristol sadly razed
As bombs fell on the city
While the holocaust still blazed.
But as the Phoenix rose again
So Bristol did as well -
New buildings, shops and houses, too,
Their modern stories tell.
The old now merges with the new
And one example to be seen
Is the Cathedral and the Council House
Both gracing College Green.

'Virtute et Industria' -
'Ship Shape and Bristol Fashion'
Are words used by Bristolians with pride -
And even passion!
Yes! Bristol is a splendid place -
It ranks amongst the best -
This city built on seven hills -
'The Gateway to the West'.

Marie Oliver

Mr And Mrs S Thompson

A new announcement of a coming together
One that brings happiness and will last forever
Kept a secret from many so you could say a shock
When he got down on one knee and produced a rock.

This man is my brother, how nervous he did look
As he raised the ring you could see how his hand shook
The small group watching all beamed with joy
My eyes filled with tears - my younger brother, no longer a wee boy.

His partner, in shock, said, 'Baby, of course I will!'
With hugs, tears and kisses, did the room fill
Now all the planning is underway
Picking dresses, kilts and flowers for the big day.

When you see them together you can see they are best friends
They would do anything for each other, even go to the world's end
The bride caused a few tears trying on a dress one day,
I promised I wouldn't, but what can I say?

Kelly really is like a sister to me
I couldn't ask for a better sister-in-law to be
Scott, not only my brother, but truly my best friend
My love for them both, it really has no end.

Their big day will be emotional but perfect in every way
It will be Mr and Mrs Thompson's, very special day.

Zoë Thompson

Out Of Control . . . Cancer

Up there in his cab he
Was
King of the Road.
At the truck stops
He would join his mates
Laugh, eat and drink
Whilst exchanging stories
And eyeing up the talent!
Now

His life was out of control
Panic
Had hitched a lift with him.
Out on the highway the
Giant wheels pounded the tarmac.
Glancing in his mirror
Life

Was fast forward.
He couldn't slam the brakes on.
Darkness . . .

No truck stops!

Julya Bukowski

Noise

Why must the public suffer noise?
Not only from the latest toys,
Out of car windows comes that beat
Each time we pause to cross the street.

Or, venture in a fashion shop,
To background of the latest pop
For deaf ears no doubt adusted,
Sound ones soon may not be trusted.

Tune in for news on BBC
It's just as bad on ITV.
Thumpy, thumpy, thumpety crash!
Percussion starts and ends the flash.

Music for dramatic effect,
Sadly, all are forced to expect
Often overrides the diction
Spoiling the attempted fiction.

It seems that supersonic booms
Have vanished from our living rooms
But, sympathy we must extend
To those who live near runways end.

Electric cables overhead
Go on humming when we're in bed,
With cancer clusters found quite near,
There's more to it than meets the ear.

Transistors, walkmen and iPods
To many have become their gods,
While mobile phones are heard to blare
At any time or anywhere.

Wailing sirens are ever near,
Emergency, sounds loud and clear.
Let mitigation be the plea,
Next time it may be you or me.

Some stressed people rely on pills
Others go walking on the hills,
Whichever way restores their poise
And conquest over demon noise.

Harry Patrick

Footsteps On The Beach

Footsteps on the beach
Each step different; unique
As we move forward to a place unknown,
We are creating history all of our own.

People try to predict the future,
Try to second guess the world of tomorrow
It is hard work and strange; worrying
Because the future is unknown.

I have watched many people try to plan their future.
Living to the do list on the kitchen table,
Struggling to fit it all in,
Turning down opportunities, because their plan says no.

We all need order and discipline,
But we also need to be undefined in our mind
Ready to recognise the mysteries in life
And those leaps of faith that fill your blood with adrenaline.

I looked at our footsteps in the sands,
Two unique prints marking out their own paths
Going in the same direction today
But neither one knows whether,
They're heading to the same destination.

Both strong individual steps; clear on their paths
Now they are learning to walk together.
Developing a new pattern whilst remaining unique
Hoping to improve the happiness of the other.

Our footsteps aren't worried about their future
As they are too busy enjoying the dance of today
Because our footsteps are creating history of our own
Giving us the strength to create a little more.

Julia Boxer

Telly Jelly

TV is a time lubricant.
It lubricates your time.

Seconds slide smoothly
From your lifespan

Whilst fictional people
Live pointless lives

In front of your eyes
Whilst you ignore yourself

Your life shoots along
In front of the glass

As you switch off the part of you
That makes you different from an animal

And switch on your modern-day
Cave fire to awe and goggle

To wilt and fade
To pale and slow
To die and rot

How many hours
Of how many days
Of how many years
Of your life

Have been lubricated
By TV?

Simon Hymers

My Boat

My boat - lovely
With delicate lines,
An anthem to speed
And Man's design.

Once more repaired,
Relaunched, she zips,
Turns, dutiful to tiller,
Delicate to the wind,
Superb on water
But ill-fated she.

Smashes, sails torn,
Sunk at moorings
And there wrecked.

Condemned to spares!

Dr Fleming Carswell

Woman II Woman

Pillow talk
You were lying
On my bed
You'd lied
Through your teeth
You lay in his arms
I thought you were straight with me.

Jenny Heasman

Life

Life moves on and people change
No matter where we are.
I can dance anywhere
Freedom's where we are, this is where we start.
Got to move on, got to stay friends forever
Got to stick together, cos life 's where we are.

Friends forever, those girls are the other half of my heart
And we sadly have to part it is so hard.

I'll never forget your simple smile
All those memories we had together
Which will slowly fade away
When we turn old and grey
But shine or rain you'll make up our day
Night or when it's light you put things right
Wherever we are, we'll think of you

And don't forget, best friends forever.

Bethany Painter (11)

Eternity

We saw sunshine on the waters
As the sea rushed to the shore;
Waves aglow with diadems and
Diamonds scattered o'er
The beauties of God's Kingdom
Displayed before our eyes,
An orchestra beyond control as God
Revealed His inner glow! Expressed
In the sea's relentless flow.

We see through a glass but darkly
Things yet beyond our grasp - with
Glimpses like this, how can we resist
The awesome bliss; of heavenly lights
Upon the deep - Revealing the One who
Never sleeps; He stands in the eternities,
Of things gone, and things to come.

Barbara Phoebe Curtis

Bloody Mary

Bloody Mary, I can see
Won't you come and live with me?
Together we can haunt the graves
And make sure every child behaves.
Through fear of being turned insane
Or never seeing day again.
Maybe they'll drop dead instead
Or have their eyes clawed from their head.
For Mary, darling, you've been hurt
And seek revenge from 'low the dirt.

Your nails, they used to be so strong
But scratching at the wood so long . . .
The coffin lid is now their bed
And from the torn up flesh you bled.
You tried to ring the graveyard bell
But from its rusty perch it fell.
In the morn your father screamed;
He'd buried you alive it seemed.
He lifted you straight from the ground
But just a bloody corpse he found.
With open eyes and sallow skin
And simple emptiness within.

Decades passed and now you're back
Your face, so scarred, is veiled in black.
And in the parallel you wait
For some poor soul to take the bait.
Whisper to the mirrored glass
And watch with fear as shadows pass.
A bell will sound and you'll arrive
Upon their pain your soul will thrive.
With you in death I long to be,
Oh Bloody Mary, come to me.

Hollie Dennison

Highgate Wood

Unmistakable the freshness of fragrances
Of pine, chestnut and honeysuckle
Welcoming as you enter by the Gypsy Gate
Revealing glimpses of a thousand and one faces.

A moment of jubilation when the sunlight
Streams in startling the plants growing
Wild in their coppiced site; silhouettes
Stretching and chasing each other in the bright
Green meadow poised in the distance.

When the sun disappears
Leaving me with the knowledge piecemeal
Of leaves and trees, daughters and mothers -

I wander into the woodland's womb
Sprawling ancient earthwork
Seeking space to replenish myself
On the floor of this weeping cathedral.

The sun reappears playing with creatures
Bursting out of their cocoons,
Negotiating a passage through the world;
The weakest learning to stand together,
The strong cherished in harmony.

The whistling and twittering of birds,
The spluttering of woodpeckers,
The wind-tickled chimes of a charm of finches
With the double rainbow renewing hope:

Est, ergo cogito: It is therefore I think.
We are what others make of us -
Pearls in a necklace, resplendent in company.

Shanta Acharya

Forward Press Information

We hope you have enjoyed reading this book
- and that you will continue to enjoy it in the
coming years.

If you like reading and writing poetry drop us a
line, or give us a call, and we'll send you a free
information pack.

Alternatively if you would like to order further copies of
this book or any of our other titles, then please give us a
call or log onto our website at www.forwardpress.co.uk

Forward Press Information
Remus House
Coltsfoot Drive
Peterborough
PE2 9JX
(01733) 890099